PEA SOUP
ANDERSEN'S
Scandinavian-American
COOKBOOK

PEA SOUP ANDERSEN'S

Scandinavian-American

COOKBOOK

Chef Ulrich Riedner

Patricia Rain
COORDINATING EDITOR

CELESTIALARTS
Berkeley, California

CELESTIAL ARTS
P.O. Box 7327
Berkeley, California 94707

Cover design by Ken Scott
Text design by Sarah Levin and Nancy Austin
Composition by Wilsted & Taylor

Library of Congress Catalog Card Number: 88-070661
ISBN 0-89087-523-5

First Printing, 1988
Manufactured in the United States of America

1   2   3   4   5—91   90   89   88

CONTENTS

ACKNOWLEDGEMENTS

I would like to thank my wife, Francine, for her help and support during the time I was working on this book, and for her recipe, Chicken with Mustard Sauce; my mother for many of the recipes that come from Germany and which I still use; Patricia Rain for her assistance on this project and for her recipe for chocolate cake; and the employees of Pea Soup Andersen's who made contributions to this book: Pam Beckworth, Theresa Bohnett, Brian Jessen, Nell Kooyman, Mary Newman, Barbara Olsen, Fernando Palomino, Joe Sanchez, Billie Thurman, and Chuck and Eileen White. Thanks also to Len Jepsen, and to Evelyn Buell for all her information on the early days of Pea Soup Andersen's, and for the use of recipes from the Ladies Presbyterian Aid Society of Santa Ynez Valley. Special thanks to Rob Andersen for his stories and helpful information.

This book is dedicated to my late brother, Helmut Riedner, who helped me develop an interest in food and cooking at a young age and who gave me loving support and assistance in my career as a chef.

FOREWORD

As this book is being published, Pea Soup Andersen's is celebrating its 64th year of serving the highway traveler in the state of California. Over four generations of families have enjoyed the hospitality of the Andersen's organization.

The story of Pea Soup Andersen's is a story of the American Dream—from roadside cafe to multiple-location corporation. It is also a tale of good citizenship, community involvement, and opportunities for employees with a wide range of ethnic backgrounds to succeed. But mainly, Pea Soup Andersen's is a story of good home-cooking, served with pride.

In writing this book, Ulrich Riedner, author and Pea Soup Andersen's corporate chef, along with Patricia Rain, coordinating editor, have combined the recipes for more than one hundred wonderful dishes with the history and stories of Pea Soup Andersen's, Buellton, and the Santa Ynez Valley.

I hope you receive many hours of enjoyment from this book.

Chuck White

Chuck White
President and Executive Officer

INTRODUCTION

T here is an old saying in Scandinavia that the Norwegians eat to live, the Swedes live to drink, and the Danes live to eat. As for us Germans, we not only live to eat, we live to eat a lot!

Food was always abundant and excellently prepared in our home and it obviously affected my brothers and me as both my elder brother and I trained as chefs in Germany, and my younger brother became involved as Restaurant Manager.

My training was primarily as a gourmet or fancy-food chef, a role which I enjoy immensely. Gourmet fare, however, is not something most of us do at home every day, especially with the demands of work and family. Fortunately, during my training I also worked in a small down-to-earth restaurant in my hometown. I learned good basic knowledge of home-cooking, something I have used often as a professional chef as well as in my own home.

The combination of gourmet *and* daily cooking has been invaluable to me working here at Pea Soup Andersen's. As you will learn as you read this book, both the Andersens were from Europe as were so many of the people who have helped to shape America's cuisine. They developed a fine reputation based on the preparation of quality home-cooked food, prepared well and served with love.

Pea Soup Andersen's grew rapidly from a small roadside cafe to a full-scale restaurant. And over the years the menus have expanded to adjust to the times and to our customers. Now, with three locations serving home-style meals as well as banquets, a full catering service, winemaker dinners, and other special events, my versatility as a chef has really begun to pay off. We may be serving breakfast in the kitchen while we are also preparing a poolside bar-b-que and an intimate gourmet dinner party featuring a Santa Ynez Valley winery. This requires that I wear several hats (or toques as we call them in the trade).

This same versatility holds true for the *Pea Soup Andersen's Cookbook*. We have attempted to give you a book that is fun to read for the fascinating history and stories, practical to use for everyday meals, and with enough panache that you will also use it for special dinners and parties. I have done my best to keep the recipes reasonably simple to prepare and with ingredients that you will already have in your home or will find in your local supermarket.

Our cookbook also contains recipes from employees at our three locations. Pea Soup Andersen's is a family restaurant, and that extends to our employees as well. They have offered recipes that have been special in their family traditions and which fit well into the Pea Soup Andersen's tradition of good wholesome meals.

The recipes in this book are made with fresh ingredients and only a minimum of packaged or prepared foods. If a recipe calls for apple-sauce, or tomato sauce, or soup stock, certainly you can use the ready-made ingredients. If you prefer, however, substitute your own freshly made sauces, soup stocks, jellies, and so forth.

That main thing is that we hope you will enjoy using this cookbook and that the recipes will be appreciated by those of you who prepare and eat the meals you create from them. I'm sure that Anton, Juliette, and Robert T. (Pea-Soup) Andersen would be delighted to know that the tradition that they started in 1924 lives on today and that people come from across the country to enjoy good cooking. I am proud to be part of this tradition and to pass it along to you in the *Pea Soup Andersen's Cookbook*.

Ulrich Riedner
Corporate Chef,
Pea Soup Andersen's

THE HISTORY OF
PEA SOUP ANDERSEN'S

On Friday, the thirteenth of June, 1924, Anton and Juliette Andersen opened the doors of their new cafe in Buellton, about 40 miles north of Santa Barbara, California. Although they certainly aspired to success, it is highly unlikely that in their wildest dreams they could have imagined the popularity their modest cafe would someday achieve, and the impact it would have on the welfare of the town of Buellton and the Santa Ynez Valley.

Anton Andersen came from Denmark, Juliette from France. They met in New York where Anton was entrenched in the restaurant business. He had been, among other things, maître d'hôtel and catering manager of world-class establishments such as the restaurants Marguerey and Voisin, Louis Sherry's, and the New York Biltmore. He and Juliette married and had Robert T. Andersen, their only child, in 1913. They came to California when the Los Angeles Biltmore opened, but Anton soon tired of the rat race (as he put it) associated with city hotels. He had a brother who had a business in Solvang, and Anton and his family made frequent trips to the Santa Ynez Valley. When the highway was diverted through Buellton in 1924 and electricity was brought to the valley, the time was right to move. The Andersens purchased a small parcel of land and a building from Mrs. R. T. Buell. They set up a cafe and brought in their prized new electric stove, the only one in the valley. Appropriately, they named their new eatery "Andersen's Electrical Cafe."

Their initial restaurant was small, consisting of six stools and a couple of booths. Instead of the elegant meals so popular in the city, they served simple, wholesome, country-style cuisine. Both Anton and Juliette were accomplished cooks, but because they catered to highway travelers, they prepared hotcakes, sandwiches, ice cream sodas, and coffee much of the time. Their first customers were the salesmen, tourists, and truck drivers who traveled the main highway between Los Angeles and San Francisco. As this was the heyday of Hearst's newspaper empire, a number of writers and reporters fre-

quented the cafe, among them Arthur Brisbane and O. O. McIntyre. These men and others praised the excellent food and hospitable atmosphere of the Electrical Cafe, and soon celebrities were stopping for a meal on their way up and down the coast. Santa Barbarans also discovered Andersen's and planned special outings to Buellton for a meal.

Although Anton did most of the short-order cooking, Juliette prepared specialties and was known for her superb French cooking. Together they tried a variety of dishes when they first opened their cafe, adopting the ones most popular with their guests. The pea soup, for which the restaurant is now so famous, wasn't served until they had been open for about three months, but it was an immediate success. The initial ten pounds of split peas were purchased from Deihl's grocery in Santa Barbara, enough for 80 bowls of soup. Then a 100-pound order was placed with William Cluff of San Francisco; within three years they placed an order for one ton of split peas from the Knoke Company in Chicago.

Faced with the dilemma of where to store a ton of peas in a small cafe, Anton finally decided to stack the bulging gunnysacks in the window. With this readily available and inexpensive advertising display, he proclaimed their restaurant "The Original Home of Split Pea Soup."

In 1928 the Andersens sank a well and built a hotel and dining room for their now quite popular cafe. They named their enlarged establishment the "Bueltmore," a play on words referring to Anton's days with the Biltmore.

Soon after the Andersens moved to the Santa Ynez Valley, they were an accepted part of the community. Juliette was a gracious woman, warm and friendly to all those around her. Anton was quite a character, but he was especially famous for his extraordinary capacity to remember faces and names without error. Once met, a person was never forgotten. This amazed anyone who ever met him, and, of course, endeared him to them as well. Apparently the young Victor Borge was among the famous people who visited Andersen's in the early days. When he would enter the cafe, the two men would let out a whoop followed by rapid-fire Danish at full volume, much to the amusement and amazement of the other customers.

Juliette was devoutly Catholic, and she and young Robert attended mass at the local mission each Sunday. The employees who lived on the Andersen property were always welcome to join them. The Andersens extended their food and friendship to the friars at the Santa Ynez Mission. Each holiday season there was a party for the brothers,

Opposite: Anton, Robert T., and Juliette standing in front of newly-opened Andersen's Electrical Cafe.

a custom that Robert continued when he took over the operation of the family business.

There were parties for the employees as well, especially at Christmas. This custom continued long after the Andersens were gone as the new owner, Vince Evans, was also very fond of giving and attending parties.

Son Robert left the Valley in 1930 to attend Stanford. After graduating, he worked on his own for a while before returning to Buellton to help run the family business. Robert was by all accounts a very "forward-looking" man, one who envisioned new and modern ways of running the business and working with food. When he returned to Buellton he established the billboards for which the restaurant became known, used Hap-Pea and Pea-Wee in advertising displays, expanded the menu, and even added special menus for children to help draw family customers, and he let the world know that Andersen's Valley Inn (a name taken during the 1930s) sold over 100,000 bowls of split pea soup a year. He even adopted his nickname, "Pea-Soup," the eventual trademark and official name of the family business.

In 1941 Pea-Soup married Rosemary Mohan. She immediately became active in the family business, and for years operated a gift shop in the upstairs of the restaurant. Their only son, Rob, was born in November of 1942.

Grand opening of wine cellar. Robert T., Juliette, son Rob, and Rosemary Andersen (left to right).

During World War II, the restaurant closed to the public. The hotel rooms were used to house military personnel stationed locally, and meals were served to servicemen and their families. Pea-Soup also purchased a small building across the street from the hotel and converted it to a canteen. The canteen was operated by the American Women's Voluntary Services (A.W.V.S.), patterned after a program begun in England. The canteen was called "Co Na Mar Corner," representing all the services: Coast Guard, Navy, Marines, and Army. The local valley members took turns providing meals for the servicemen on weekends.

After the war, Pea-Soup

Andersen's Valley Inn circa 1940.

reopened the restaurant with a flourish. He commissioned Milt Neil
to draw new cartoon characters for Hap-Pea and Pea-Wee, and a contest was held to name the two characters. The cartoon figures moved
into the limelight and added to the draw of the customers stopping for
meals and a place to spend the night. The dining area was dramati-
cally enlarged. In 1947 the name of the restaurant was changed to
"Pea Soup Andersen's," the name that has remained to the present. At
the same time Buellton was nicknamed "The Home of Split Pea
Soup," a name they are still proud of today.

In the late 1940s Pea-Soup developed frozen pea soup, which was an
immediate success when it came onto the market. Creating a quality
canned pea soup was a little more difficult, but in 1951 Pea-Soup
invented a process that made the canned soup taste almost as fresh as
the frozen. In 1954 Heublein Company bought the soup company,
which is now owned by Real Fresh in Visalia.

In 1947 the Coast highway was rerouted through the center of
Buellton. Although the town businesses were forced to give up 20 feet
of their property for the new highway, they felt it was worthwhile—it
would bring further fame to the small town of Buellton as it catered
to the needs of highway travelers.

Over the years the business continued to grow. Each year something new was introduced or changed to allow for the expansion of
the business and the popularity of the restaurant. In 1958 Pea-Soup
introduced a line of Danish wines that are still imported today from
the same small town in Denmark. In 1959 the Hans Christian Andersen Cocktail Lounge was built, complete with the fairy-tale mural
painted by Santa Ynez Valley artist Paul Kuelgen. During the festivi-
ties in June, Pea-Soup said, "When the remodeling is completed, we'll
have the same clean, wholesome family atmosphere as before, but
we'll be larger, newer, and better able to serve everyone." This pledge
of integrity has been a key theme of Pea Soup Andersen's for all the
years it has served the public.

In the early 1960s, Pea-Soup decided to open restaurants in Santa

Maria and Salinas. After a few years, however, Pea-Soup decided he needed a break from the high-paced family business, and in April of 1965, the Buellton restaurant was sold to Vince Evans. The other two locations were later sold to Denny's Corporation.

The new owner of Pea Soup Andersen's, Vince Evans, was a larger-than-life personality, well known and already established as a leader in the Santa Ynez Valley. At the end of World War II, Vince began a career in acting and developed a close friendship with fellow actor

Vince Evans.

Ronald Reagan, who later purchased a ranch in the Santa Ynez Valley. Vince and his wife Margery moved to a 900-acre ranch south of Buellton in 1959. They raised cattle, and he operated a feed store and grew alfalfa. When he bought Pea Soup Andersen's, he jumped into his newest endeavor with the same high energy and enthusiasm that he displayed for his many other ventures.

The business thrived under Evans's hand. In 1967 the Valley Room was added, and by then the restaurant was purchasing 50 tons of split peas each year, enough for three-quarters of a million bowls of soup!

Vince had a shrewd eye for promotion. One year he had Lassie come to visit Buellton; another year, elephants and clowns at Christmas. He built an aviary and filled it with parrots, and he installed a train for children that went from the restaurant to the area where the motel now stands. He even had a miniature wild animal park for two years, filled with just about everything but giraffes.

The wild animal park was discontinued when the kitchen was modernized and a parking lot was built to make way for the addition of a Danish-style motel built in 1970.

The Evanses were very active with the Santa Barbara Symphony. They provided the valley with the Andersen's Symphony van, which toured county schools to introduce children in the valley to the symphony and the musical instruments played. He also was constantly supporting children in the valley with their 4-H projects.

Vince took an interest in his employees as well. One employee in particular, Fernando Palomino, became like a son to Evans. Fernando had come to the United States speaking no English when he was 17 years old. When he came to Pea Soup Andersen's in 1965, he worked split shifts at the restaurant while learning English at a local high school. When his English was good, he enrolled in college. He convinced the management to let him become a waiter. When Vince bought the restaurant, the staff was nervous about waiting on his table, so Fernando volunteered. Soon Vince made Fernando his personal waiter. Over time, Vince moved Fernando through the various positions in the restaurant until he was made assistant manager. By the time Vince purchased and remodeled the large Sierra-style restaurant and saloon at Mammoth Lakes in 1973, Fernando came in as a business partner. And in 1975, Vince and Fernando again collaborated, this time in the building of Pea Soup Andersen's in Santa Nella, an enormously successful venture.

In 1979 Vince purchased an English pub that had stood for over 100 years at the Liverpool railway station in London. The pub was reconstructed in Buellton and opened as a bar and entertainment center. Also in 1979, Vince decided to build yet another Pea Soup Andersen's—this time in Carlsbad, just north of San Diego.

Vince had expansive dreams and the energy to make the dreams a reality. Unfortunately, neither dreams nor energy could change the cards fate dealt him. On April 23, 1980, Vince, his wife Marge, and their 21-year-old daughter, Venetia, were tragically killed in a small plane crash just minutes from the Santa Ynez Valley airport.

Needless to say, everyone at Pea Soup Andersen's, as well as the Santa Ynez Valley, was shocked and saddened by the news. The business was taken over by the Evans estate with the Bank America Trust Department acting as trustee. The business was later purchased by Pea Soup Properties Limited in 1983.

Pea Soup Andersen's survived the hard times in the early 1980s and is now growing stronger and larger each year. Led by a skilled team of professionals in business management, as well as highly competent office support, marketing, advertising, and sales staff, and restaurant and hotel employees, Pea Soup Andersen's continues to thrive.

Based on the same quality food, service, and accommodations established by Anton, Juliette, and Robert T., Pea Soup Andersen's has adapted to accommodate the changing needs of both travelers and locals who frequent the three sites. Each year the number of visitors coming to Pea Soup Andersen's grows, bringing the yearly total of the three locations to 1.5 million visitors, who eat an average of 1,752,000 bowls of split pea soup.

Though the times and the number of visitors have certainly changed, the pea soup has remained the same. Anton, Juliette, and Robert T. would certainly be proud if they could see what became of their Andersen's Electrical Cafe!

COOKING TERMS AND TIPS

BAKE: To cook, covered or uncovered, by dry heat (usually in an oven).

BAR-B-QUE: Has different meanings, but generally applies to food roasted over an open fire, often on a grill. Also, a spicy, smoky sauce.

BASTE: Brush or spoon liquid over food while it cooks to keep the food moist and to add flavor.

BOUILLON: Clear soup stock made from fish, meat or poultry bones, or vegetables.

DREDGE: To coat food well, usually with flour.

DRIPPINGS: Fat or juices from cooked meats or poultry.

FRY: To cook in hot oil or other fats.

GARNISH: To decorate a completed dish of food.

MARINADE: A seasoned liquid usually containing spices, herbs, oil, and/or wine, in which foods soak to tenderize and to add flavor.

MARINATE: To soak in a marinade.

MINCE: To chop finely.

POACH: To cook in liquid, just below the boiling point (simmer).

ROAST: To cook meat or poultry, covered or uncovered, by dry heat (usually in an oven). Also, a cut of meat cooked in this way.

ROUX: Mixture of fat and flour, used for thickening, and cooked until bubbly.

SAUTÉ: Cook or brown over heat in a small amount of oil or butter (panfry).

SEAR: Brown surface of food over high heat quickly to seal in juices.

STALK: An individual piece, as in one stalk (rib) of celery.

This book is intended as a guide to good cooking and eating. Almost all the recipes can be adjusted, depending upon ingredients you have available, your taste, dietary restrictions, and so on. When I am cooking a meal or dish, I do not think in terms of tablespoons or cups. I automatically add more liquid to dilute a sauce to the proper consistency or I might cook down a sauce to thicken it. The best test is in the tasting. If it requires something, add to it; if it's good, leave it alone.

Exact measurements are not important in dishes such as soups, stews, roasts, and sauces. In baking, however, all recipes should be followed exactly for best results.

SMØRREBRØD

O ne of the great specialties of Denmark is the *smørrebrød*, or open-faced sandwiches. The Danes love variety and believe in exciting as well as satisfying the appetite, so as you can imagine, the *smørrebrød* is very popular.

In Scandinavia there are restaurants that specialize in the *smørrebrød*. The waiter presents the guests with a *smørrebrødsseddel* (literally "buttered bread slip"). The guests mark the menu to indicate their selections. The waiter then totals the bill and places the slips with the kitchen. Usually the *smørrebrødsseddel* is returned to the guests when the sandwiches are served so that they can check to make sure they have received what was ordered.

The following is a sample of a *smørrebrødseddel*. We'd like to suggest you use it as a guide for making special sandwiches. In fact, you might consider having a sandwich buffet party for family or friends. Offer several varieties of breads, meats, condiments, spreads, and garnishes, and your guests can be as creative as they wish.

SMØRREBRØDSSEDDEL

	Price	Black Bread	Rye Bread	White Bread	Whole Wheat	Pumper-nickel
Caviar						
Smoked Goosebreast						
Gooseliver Paté						
FISH						
Lobster (fresh)						
Lobster (fresh) with mayonnaise						
Shrimp, single layer						
Shrimp, double layer						
Roasted Plaice with Remoulade Sauce						
Roasted Hake						
Smoked Salmon Lox						
Crab Meat						
Crab Legs						
Smoked Salmon Lox with Egg						
Smoked Eel						
Smoked Eel with Egg						
Sardines						
Sardines with Tomatoes						
Boneless Herring						
Marinated Herring						
Smoked Herring						
Smoked Herring with Egg						
MEATS						
Roasted Veal with Dill Pickles						
Steak Tartare with Onions						

SMØRREBRØDSSEDDEL cont.

	Price	Black Bread	Rye Bread	White Bread	Whole Wheat	Pumper-nickel
Steak Tartare with Onions and Egg						
Boiled Beef with Horseradish						
Boiled Beef with Mixed Pickles						
Boiled Beef with Cucumbers						
Roast Beef with Horseradish						
Roast Beef with Remoulade Sauce						
Beefsteak with Onions						
Beefsteak with Onion and Egg						
Corned Beef						
Beef Tongue						
Frikadeller with Dill Pickles						
Smoked Pork Fillets						
Smoked Cured Ham						
Smoked Baked Ham						
Smoked Baked Ham and Egg						
Roasted Pork Loin						
Liverwurst						
Salami						
Tongue Sausage						
Venison Steak with Aspic						
SALADS						
Italian Salad						
Herringsalad with Egg						

SMØRREBRØDSSEDDEL cont.

	Price	Black Bread	Rye Bread	White Bread	Whole Wheat	Pumper-nickel
Shrimp Salad						
Russian Salad						
Meat Salad						
Liver Paté						
Liver Paté with Pickles						
Eggs and Sardines						
Eggs and Boneless Herring						
Chopped Egg and Herring						
Sliced Tomatoes						
Sliced Tomatoes with Egg						
Sliced Tomatoes with Sardines						
CHEESE						
Gruyere						
Camembert						
Gorgonzola						
Roquefort						
Danish Blue Cheese						
Swiss						
Danish						
Tilsit						
Gouda						
Costello						
Creme Danica						

Waiter: _____   Date: _____   Pieces: _____

Bill Number: _____   Total Amount: _____

SOUPS

The split peas we use in Andersen's split pea soup are from the rolling Palouse Hills region of eastern Washington and northern Idaho, a band of land 250 miles long and 50 miles wide. There are about 2,000 growers of dry peas in the United States, *all* of whom live and work in this area.

Split peas don't grow that way naturally. They come three to four in a pod and are allowed to dry on the vine. When they are harvested and processed to steam off the seed coat, the peas split along their natural seam. By removing the seed coat and having the peas split, they cook very quickly. They need no soaking, and, once brought to a boil, they will cook to tenderness in about 30 minutes.

Split peas are an almost perfect food. They are high in fiber, protein, potassium, and complex carbohydrates. There is more protein per pound in split peas than there is in beef steak, and no cholesteral besides! And there is as much fiber in an 8-oz. bowl of split pea soup as there is in one large ripe apple.

Best of all, split pea soup tastes good—good enough to sell at least 4,800 bowls of split pea soup at Andersen's every day!

Here is the pea soup recipe that made Andersen's so famous. It was one of Juliette's recipes that she tested with the customers after the cafe was open for about three months. It's ironic that the soup that made a Danish restaurant so famous came originally from France. Regardless of its origin, it is truly delicious.

PEA SOUP ANDERSEN'S ORIGINAL PEA SOUP RECIPE

2 quarts of soft water
2 cups of Andersen's specially
   selected green split peas
1 stalk of celery, coarsely
   chopped
1 large carrot, chopped
1 small onion, chopped
¼ teaspoon ground thyme
1 pinch of cayenne pepper
1 bay leaf, ground
salt and pepper to taste

Combine all ingredients in a big pot. Bring to a boil, and boil hard for 20 minutes, then simmer until peas are tender. Strain through a fine sieve and then reheat to boiling point.

Recipe serves 6 to 8 bowls of Andersen's split pea soup.

Needless to say, we no longer prepare Andersen's split pea soup in quantities like those Juliette first prepared. In fact, we prepare the soup by the tank-full, and frequently we prepare six tanks of split pea soup at each location in one day. To give you an idea of how much the recipe has grown, here is the same recipe geared to serve 850 bowls of Andersen's split pea soup.

80 gallons soft water
160 pounds Andersen's specially
   selected green split peas
15 pounds celery, coarsely
   chopped
15 pounds carrots, chopped
15 pounds onions, chopped
3 tablespoons ground thyme
3 tablespoons cayenne pepper
3 tablespoons ground bay leaves
3 tablespoons white pepper
2 pounds salt

Prepare soup as on previous page, and invite your neighbors in for soup!

As this is a Scandinavian-American cookbook, and as its story is based around peas, we have included a few variations on the pea soup theme. The following three recipes were supplied to us by the Idaho-Washington Dry Pea Commission.

DANISH CREAMY SPLIT PEA SOUP

1 cup split peas
1 tablespoon butter or oil
½ cup chopped onion
½ cup chopped celery
½ cup chopped turnip
2 slices (1 to 2 ounces) ham or
  turkey ham, sliced
½ teaspoon dried marjoram
  leaves, crumbled
dash nutmeg
dash white pepper
1 quart chicken stock, broth, or
  bouillon
½ cup dairy sour cream
½ to 1 teaspoon horseradish
½ to 1 teaspoon sugar

In a large saucepan or soup pot sauté vegetables in butter or oil until just tender, about 5 to 8 minutes. Add peas, meat, seasonings, and stock. Heat to boiling, reduce heat to simmer. Cover and simmer just until peas are soft, about 30 minutes. Pour soup into blender or food processor and blend until smooth, or put through food mill. Blend sour cream, horseradish, and sugar. Top each serving with a dollop of horseradish cream.

4 servings.

HOW MUCH PEA SOUP
CAN A TRUE PEA-SOUPER EAT?

It has always been customary at Pea Soup Andersen's to offer hungry travelers as much split pea soup as they can eat. The delicious soup and fresh bread, always hearty and satisfying, is often eaten for breakfast as well as lunch and dinner by pea soup fans. Many of our guests eat three or four bowls of pea soup in one sitting.

Occasionally, however, we have had customers who have chosen to take the all-you-can-eat offer one step further to just how much pea soup can a true pea-souper eat?

The record number of bowls of pea soup eaten in one sitting was held by a Stanford student after a session at at a table at Andersen's in 1952: fourteen bowls of pea soup! The title held until September of 1969, when seventeen-year-old Sam Johnson, a Santa Ynez Valley football player and heavyweight wrestler, decided to challenge the old record. Johnson, who was also student-body president of the Santa Ynez Valley High School that year, sat down and ate SIXTEEN BOWLS OF ANDERSEN'S PEA SOUP! Johnson weighed 235 pounds before soup time; he said afterward that he felt ten pounds heavier, which is not far off from accurate. In fact, the big bowls of pea soup at Andersen's are twelves ounces each; sixteen bowls meant he weighed twelve pounds more after supper than before—assuming he didn't eat bread with the soup. Rumor has it that when Johnson walked, he could be heard sloshing for days afterward.

We don't recommend people stretch the limits of their imaginations—or their waistlines—to this extent. We encourage people to eat as much pea soup as they wish, but sixteen bowls. . . .

SPLIT PEA SOUP MILANO

1 cup split peas
5 cups water
5 bouillon cubes
dash pepper
1/4 pound Italian sausage
1 cup chopped celery
1/2 cup chopped onion
1 clove garlic, minced
1/2 cup sweet red pepper, minced
1/4 cup dry red wine
grated Parmesan cheese, for
   garnish

In a large saucepan or pot combine peas, water, bouillon cubes, and pepper. Heat to boiling, reduce heat to simmer. Cover and simmer until peas are tender, stirring occasionally, about 30 minutes.

Meanwhile, in skillet over medium heat, cook sausage until no longer pink, breaking it into small pieces with the back of a spoon.

Add celery, onion, garlic, and pepper, and sauté until onion is tender and translucent, about 5 minutes.

Add sausage-vegetable mixture to peas along with wine and simmer 10 to 15 minutes to blend flavors.

Sprinkle each serving with Parmesan cheese.

4 to 6 servings.

SPLIT PEA SOUP SANTA FE

1 cup split peas
1 tablespoon oil
½ cup chopped onion
¼ cup chopped celery
1 or 2 cloves garlic, minced
1 quart beef stock, broth, or
    bouillon
1 or 2 small whole hot red
    peppers
½ teaspoon oregano
½ teaspoon ground cumin
½ teaspoon ground coriander
fresh cilantro, for garnish

In a large saucepan or soup pot, sauté onion, celery, and garlic in oil until tender, about 5 minutes. Add peas, stock, and seasonings, and heat to boiling.

Reduce heat to simmer. Cover and simmer until peas are tender, about 30 minutes. Remove hot peppers.

Garnish with fresh cilantro leaves.

4 servings.

Early soup ad.

DANISH POTATO SOUP

½ cup onion, chopped fine
½ cup celery, chopped fine
½ cup carrots, chopped fine
3 cups potatoes, sliced thin
1 tablespoon butter
1 bay leaf
⅛ teaspoon ground thyme
2 quarts chicken stock
chopped chives for garnish
salt and pepper to taste

In a large saucepan or kettle sauté onion, celery, and carrots lightly in butter. Add potatoes, chicken stock, bay leaf, and thyme.

Cook slowly for 30 to 40 minutes, or until potatoes are well done.

Adjust seasonings to taste and sprinkle with chopped chives when serving.

6 to 8 servings.

I like my creamed soups rich in flavor and very smooth. After the soup is done, add 1 tablespoon fresh butter and work into soup with a whisk. Keep hot, but don't boil or the soup may separate.

CREAM OF MUSHROOM SOUP

½ pound fresh mushrooms, chopped fine
3 tablespoons butter
2 tablespoons flour
1 tablespoon onion, chopped fine
1 cup chicken stock, hot
2 cups milk
½ cup heavy cream
¼ teaspoon salt
⅛ teaspoon white pepper
⅛ teaspoon ground thyme
1 small bay leaf
1 dash Worcestershire sauce (optional)
parsley or chopped scallions for garnish

Wash and chop mushrooms. Sauté in butter along with onion, until soft. Do not brown. Blend in the flour, stirring until smooth. Cook for 5 minutes.

Add the hot chicken stock, stir, and simmer until thickened. Add seasonings and milk, and simmer for 5 minutes.

Lower heat and add cream. Do not boil.

Garnish each bowl with a sprinkling of parsley or chopped scallions if desired.

Minestrone soup is basically a great vegetable soup with an Italian name. The vegetables used can be adapted to fit the season. Fresh spinach is especially good in this soup. Add 5 minutes before serving.

MINESTRONE SOUP

1 cup dry white beans such as
  Great Northern or Navy
  beans, soaked overnight
3 quarts salted water
1 tablespoon olive oil
2 ounces salt pork or 3 slices
  bacon, cut into small pieces
1 garlic clove, chopped fine
1 small onion, chopped
½ cup celery, chopped
½ cup carrots, diced
1 small turnip, peeled and diced
1 cup cabbage, shredded
2 small zucchini or other
  summer squash, diced
3 tomatoes, peeled, seeded, and
  chopped
1 tablespoon tomato paste
1 teaspoon basil, chopped, or ½
  teaspoon dried basil,
  crumbled
1 teaspoon oregano, chopped, or
  ½ teaspoon dried oregano,
  crumbled
1 tablespoon parsley, chopped
1 cup macaroni
salt and freshly ground black
  pepper to taste
2 quarts water or chicken stock
6 tablespoons Parmesan cheese,
  grated

Drain the beans and boil in salted water until tender, about 1 hour. Drain.

Place olive oil in large kettle. Add pork (or bacon), garlic, onion, parsley, basil, and oregano, and sauté lightly.

Add tomato paste, celery, carrots, turnips, cabbage, zucchini, tomatoes, boiled beans water (or stock), salt and pepper. Simmer 30 minutes or until vegetables are tender.

Add the macaroni and cook 10 minutes until tender.

Adjust seasonings. Sprinkle Parmesan cheese over each portion when served.

In Europe we enjoy a fruit soup served either hot or cold before the main course. In the summer it reminds us that summer has finally come again, and in the winter, it helps us get through the long, dark months. Berries, cherries, and plums are our favorite fruits for fruit soups, but apples, pears, and oranges are sometimes used as well. You can substitute other fruits for the berries if you wish.

FRUIT SOUP

1 pound berries (2 pints), washed and stemmed
1 cup water
1 cup dry white wine
¼ cup sugar
2 tablespoons lemon juice
1 tablespoon cornstarch with
2 tablespoons cold water blended in
½ teaspoon cinnamon
pinch of nutmeg
heavy cream or sour cream

Simmer berries in water for 10 to 15 minutes, or until mushy. Puree in a blender until smooth.

Return to the saucepan and add remaining ingredients. Heat to boiling, stirring frequently. Boil for 2 to 3 minutes.

Serve hot or chilled with a tablespoon of heavy cream or sour cream topping each serving.

2 to 4 servings.

This is a dessert soup, though some people serve it as a first course. Don't be misled by the word "soup." It is a very refreshing dish to serve as a dessert.

CHERRY WINE SOUP

1½ cups water
¼ cup honey
2 pounds dark sweet cherries, pitted
½ teaspoon lemon rind, grated
½ teaspoon orange rind, grated
1 cinnamon stick
2 tablespoons cornstarch with 3 tablespoons water
1½ cups sweet red wine
whipped cream

Put first six ingredients in a large saucepan. Bring to a boil and simmer for 10 minutes, until cherries are tender.

Add cornstarch blended with water. Simmer for 2 to 3 minutes.

Pour in wine, remove cinnamon stick, and chill.

Serve cold, garnished with whipped cream.

Serves 4 to 6.

HISTORICAL FACTS ABOUT THE HUMBLE PEA

- According to archeologists and ethno-botanists, peas were among the first plants domesticated.

- The oldest peas discovered are from the "spirit caves" on the border between Burma and Thailand. The peas were carbon-dated at 9700 B.C.

- It has been generally assumed that peas originated in the Near East. Actually they probably originated closer to India, as the word "pea" is believed to have come from Sanskrit.

- The oldest peas in the Near East were found at Jarmo, in northeastern Iraq, and are ascribed to the 6th or 7th millenium B.C., at least 2,000 years after the Burmese discovery.

- Charred remains of peas have been found in tombs in Egypt. These were probably "oasis" peas, a small, wild pea adapted to growing in hotter climates than the peas from which our domesticated peas now come.

- Hot pea soup was sold on the streets of Athens at the time of Pericles.

- Apicus had a number of recipes for peas in his cookbook (an early best-seller).

- The peas in early Greece and Rome were usually used dried.

- Peas were a big item during the Dark Ages. They were inexpensive and could be stored for times of food shortage or famine. Harsh penalties were inflicted on anyone caught damaging pea crops or stealing peas from fields.

- Charlemagne ordered peas to be planted in his vast holdings in 800 A.D.

- Pease Porridge (as in Pease Porridge Hot, Pease Porridge Cold) was actually a very thick pea soup. It was served in the early soup kitchens for the homeless and hungry.

- The cultivated peas we like best didn't exist before the Italian Renaissance. Until the 1400s peas were only used dried. When the "piselli novelli" was introduced, peas were finally eaten fresh.

- *Peas were a popular Lenten dish in Merry Old England. An Elizabethan writer wrote, "Peas and leeks are boiled in Lent."*

- *None other than Christopher Columbus was supposed to have brought peas to the New World. He allegedly planted them on Isabella Island in 1493.*

- *The Native Americans thought peas were a terrific addition to their lives, unlike some of the other gifts from the Europeans.*

- *The first peas in New England were planted in 1602 by an early American explorer, Captain Bartholomew Gosnold, on Cuttyhunk Island.*

- *The British, always orderly, were the first to develop and cat-alogue varieties of peas, many of which they named after royalty.*

- *Thomas Jefferson, whose Monticello Farm was famous for the quality and variety of its produce, was quite fond of peas. He grew 30 different varieties.*

- *Early American settlers almost always carried peas with them as they traveled west, both to eat on the way, and to plant when they arrived at their destination.*

- *In 1866 the Austrian monk Gregor Johann Mendel published* Experiments on Plant Hybrids, *which explained how investi-gations with garden peas show that specific traits are passed on by discrete units known as genes. This is why you look as you do whereas I tend to look more like me.*

- *Today nearly 95 percent of the nation's supply of dry split peas are grown in the rolling hills of eastern Washington and Northern Idaho. Seventy-five percent of the annual U.S. crop is sold abroad, to almost every region of the world.*

- *Despite the quantity of peas exported elsewhere, approxi-mately 69,880 pounds are bought each year from Moscow, Idaho, by none other than Pea Soup Andersen's. This pur-chase gives Pea Soup Andersen's the distinction of being the largest single split pea purchaser in the world!*

Anton, Juliette, and Robert T. Andersen (left to right) upon arriving in 1924.

SALADS & APPETIZERS

Herring is a very common European dish—so common that it is easy to find jars of herring in most supermarkets in the United States for families from Europe and their descendents. This is my favorite way of preparing it. It can be served as an appetizer or as a luncheon or light supper entree. Serve with dark pumpernickel or rye bread.

HERRING IN SOUR CREAM

1 pound jar wine herring
1 large red apple
1 medium dill pickle, cut
   lengthwise in half, then sliced
   thin
1 small onion thinly sliced into
   1-inch strips
1/4 cup mayonnaise
1/3 cup sour cream
1/8 teaspoon salt (or to taste)
1/8 teaspoon white pepper (or to
   taste)
1/2 teaspoon Worcestershire
   sauce
1 tablespoon chives or green
   onion, chopped (for garnish)

Place mayonnaise, sour cream, salt, pepper, and Worcestershire sauce into a medium-size bowl and mix well.

Peel, quarter, core, and slice apples into 1/8-inch pieces. Mix in with dressing along with pickle, onion, and herring. Mix gently until all ingredients are covered with dressing. Refrigerate for two to four hours.

Serve on lettuce leaves and sprinkle with chives or green onion.

4 appetizer-sized servings.

This version of herring isn't quite so rich as the first.

SHERRY HERRING

4 herring
1 onion, chopped
1 tablespoon dried dill weed
   (2 tablespoons fresh)
¼ cup sherry
½ cup tomato juice
1 to 2 tablespoons sugar
½ teaspoon allspice

Cut herring into 1 to 2 inch pieces. Combine with onion and dill weed.
   Combine sherry, juice, sugar, and allspice. Pour over herring.

DANISH CHEESE SPREAD

3 ounces Danish cream cheese
4 ounces Danbo or Tybo cheese,
   grated
3 tablespoons ketchup
1 tablespoon cream
2 tablespoons chopped green
   pepper
1 tablespoon green onion,
   chopped
¼ teaspoon Worcestershire
   sauce

Run ingredients through blender or food processor until smooth, adding more cream if necessary to make more spreadable.
   Serve with good crackers or bread.

Customers often wonder about how much soup we serve at Pea Soup Andersen's. We can always guarantee our customers that we make our pea soup fresh every day. The truth is we make it several times a day! As you'll see from the following Pea Soup Facts, we go through a lot of soup—and a lot of peas—keeping our customers satisfied at our three locations.

- Pea Soup Andersen's serves 6 80-gallon tanks of split pea soup per day on slow days. On busy days, 18 80-gallon tanks are served.

- Each tank contains 160 pounds of split peas.

- On the average, Pea Soup Andersen's serves 960 gallons of split pea soup every day, using 1,920 pounds of split peas each day.

- Each gallon serves approximately 10½ bowls of split pea soup. Each tank serves 853 bowls of split pea soup.

- On the average, Pea Soup Andersen's serves 4,800 bowls of pea soup every day.

- In every gallon of split pea soup, there are 2 pounds of dry split peas. Therefore there are 3.2 ounces of dry split peas in every 12-ounce bowl of soup.

- Pea Soup Andersen's buys 13,440 pounds of dry split peas from Moscow, Idaho, each week. That means Pea Soup Andersen's purchases 69,880 pounds of dry split peas every year from Moscow, Idaho, home of the National Dry Pea and Lentil Commission. Not only are there a lot of satisfied customers, but there are a lot of satisfied pea growers because of Pea Soup Andersen's!

Celery root salad is a very common European dish, especially around the winter holidays. We always had celery root salad near Christmas, with a main dish served at the same time.

CELERY ROOT SALAD

2 celery roots*
2 to 3 quarts water
2 to 3 tablespoons vinegar
1 tablespoon salt

DRESSING

½ cup olive oil or salad oil
3 tablespoons white vinegar
1 tablespoon onion, chopped
    fine
1 teaspoon parsley, chopped fine
salt and freshly ground black
    pepper

Clean the celery roots under running water, then cook, covered, in the boiling water with vinegar and salt added, until tender.

Cool, peel, and slice into thin strips or slices.

Combine slices of celery root with the dressing, and mix well.

Allow salad to sit in the refrigerator overnight before serving.

4 to 6 servings.

*Celery roots are available in most groceries at certain times of the year. If necessary, ask your grocer to order them for you.

PEA SALAD

2 cups cooked peas, chilled
¾ cup diced red bell pepper
4 ounces marinated mushrooms
2 tablespoons sliced green onion
¼ cup sour cream
2 tablespoons mayonnaise
1 tablespoon chopped fresh dill
¼ teaspoon Worcestershire
   sauce

Combine peas, red bell peppers, mushrooms, and green onion in a medium-size bowl.

In a small bowl combine remaining ingredients, mixing well. Toss with the vegetables.

Cover bowl and chill in refrigerator for at least one hour before serving.

Serves 4.

PICKLED BEETS

10 small beets

DRESSING

1 cup cider vinegar
4 tablespoons water
4 tablespoons sugar
1 pinch ground cloves
1 small onion, sliced fine
   (optional)

Cut tops off beets, leaving about 1 inch of stem and the root ends. This prevents the beets from bleeding.

Cook beets in salted water for 15 to 20 minutes or until tender.

Cool, peel, and cut into thin slices. Place in a glass dish and pour dressing over beets.

Allow to stand 2 to 3 hours before serving.

If canned beets are used, drain beet juice and pour dressing over beets.

6 servings.

Mushroom salads seem to be one of the first items to disappear on a buffet, so you may want to make double portions of the following salad if you want any for yourself.

MUSHROOM SALAD WITH CREAMY MUSTARD DRESSING

¾ to 1 pound fresh mushrooms, ideally small button mushrooms
salt and freshly ground pepper
2 to 3 tablespoons white wine vinegar
1 cup sour cream
1 tablespoon lemon juice
2 tablespoons finely minced parsley
1 clove garlic, finely minced (optional)
2 teaspoons Dijon-style mustard

Trim mushroom stems flat to mushroom caps. Wipe the caps with a damp paper towel and slice thinly unless they are very small. Place in a serving bowl and sprinkle with salt, pepper, and vinegar. Allow mushrooms to marinate for an hour.

Mix the remainder of the ingredients in a small bowl.

Drain the mushrooms and pour the mustard sauce over them. Blend well and adjust seasonings to taste.

Chill for 2 to 4 hours before serving.

Barbara Olsen, of Pea Soup Andersen's in Buellton, has a great salad recipe for banquets and buffets. With increased interest in broccoli (a very good anti-cancer vegetable), guests will certainly appreciate this salad.

BROCCOLI AND MUSHROOM SALAD

1 large bunch broccoli, cleaned and cut into bite-sized pieces
1 pound mushrooms, cleaned and sliced
2 bunches of scallions (green onions)

DRESSING

1 cup olive oil or salad oil
½ cup red wine vinegar
½ cup sugar
1 teaspoon celery seeds
1 teaspoon salt
1 teaspoon paprika
1 teaspoon onion powder

Put vegetables in a large bowl. Cover completely with dressing, mixing well.

Refrigerate for several hours before serving to allow flavors to blend well.

DANISH MACARONI SALAD

1 cup cooked peas
1 cup carrots, diced and cooked
3 cups macaroni, cooked
1 pound ham, sliced into strips
1 medium dill pickle, sliced into
   strips
1 medium onion, chopped fine
1½ cups mayonnaise
1 tablespoon parsley, chopped
1 tablespoon fresh dill, chopped
1 tablespoon white vinegar
salt and pepper to taste
2 hard-boiled eggs and 2
   tomatoes for garnish

Place peas, carrots, macaroni, ham, pickle, and onion into a salad bowl. In a small bowl mix together mayonnaise, parsley, dill, vinegar, and salt and pepper.

Stir the dressing into the salad and let it marinate for 1 to 2 hours.

Garnish with sliced eggs and tomato wedges.

What is a picnic without potato salad? This salad is best if prepared a day in advance—so that the potatoes will absorb the flavor of the dressing.

POTATO SALAD

2 pounds potatoes (about 8
   medium potatoes)
1 rib of celery, diced small
1 onion, chopped
1 hard-boiled egg, chopped
1 small dill pickle, chopped
   with about 2 tablespoons of
   the juice reserved for dressing
¼ cup white vinegar
½ cup mayonnaise
1 tablespoon salad mustard
½ teaspoon white pepper
1 teaspoon salt
1 tablespoon diced pimento
1 tablespoon parsley, chopped

Cook potatoes in salted water until fork-tender, about 30 minutes.

Drain, peel, and cut into ¼-inch slices, or dice them into ½-inch cubes. Place in a large bowl.

In another bowl, combine all other ingredients and mix well. Pour over potatoes and toss lightly until all the potatoes have been coated with dressing.

4 to 6 servings.

This is from the original cartoon by the artist Forbell (see story next page).

THE STORY OF HAP-PEA AND PEA-WEE

The well-known characters, Hap-Pea and Pea-Wee, did not spring to life with the opening of the Electrical Cafe or even Andersen's Valley Inn. They, like most of us, were a transplant from another place, in this case, from the pen of Forbell, a famous cartoonist of the 1920s. Forbell penned the large jolly mallet swinger and his serious little helper as part of a series of cartoons entitled "Little Known Occupations." One of these occupations was splitting peas for split pea soup. The chefs are shown hard at work splitting peas that are dropped down a chute in a big soup kitchen.

The cartoon appeared in the old Judge magazine; when some family member or friend saw it, the cartoon was cut out and hung on the wall. Later the Andersen family got permission from the artist to use the two characters as their trademark and the peasplitters appeared on billboard signs and other advertising for the restaurant.

Around 1944 Robert T. (Pea-Soup) Andersen commissioned Milt Neil, a Disney-trained artist, to redraw the characters from the original cartoon and to give them each a distinctive personality. In the new cartoon, the big fellow is getting the glory and the easy work, and the little one is nervous, sad, and a little frightened, always in danger of the mallet. By comparing the cartoon on p. 43 with the one shown below, you will see how the appearance of the two characters evolved.

In April of 1946 a contest was held to name the characters. From thousands of entries, the names "Hap-Pea" and "Pea-Wee" were chosen. At the award ceremony in Buellton the winner collected the $100 prize by splitting a huge concrete pea, inside of which awaited the money.

HAP-PEA

PEA-WEE

HOT POTATO SALAD

2 pounds potatoes
6 slices bacon cut into thin
    strips
2 medium onions, chopped
2 teaspoons flour
1 tablespoon sugar
¼ teaspoon pepper
1 teaspoon salt
1 cup water
⅓ cup vinegar (cider or white)
1 tablespoon parsley, chopped
1 tablespoon pimentos

Boil potatoes in salted water until fork-tender (25 to 30 minutes). Drain, peel, and slice into ¼-inch-thick slices.

In a large skillet cook bacon until crisp. Remove bacon, add onions to drippings, and sauté until tender (do not brown).

Blend in flour, sugar, pepper, and salt. Gradually add water and vinegar. Simmer for 5 minutes.

Add potatoes, bacon, pimentos, and parsley, and toss lightly to coat with dressing.

Serve hot.

WARM (WILTED) SPINACH SALAD

1 pound (2 to 3 bunches) fresh
   spinach
1 small red onion, sliced thin
6 strips of bacon, diced
freshly ground black pepper

DRESSING

1 cup water
½ cup sugar
¼ cup red wine vinegar
½ teaspoon salt
2 tablespoons lemon juice
   (about ½ lemon)

Wash the spinach well in water, trimming away all stems and browned pieces. Drain the spinach leaves well, then tear into bite-sized pieces.

Place spinach in a large bowl. Top with the sliced onions.

In a small saucepan boil the water and sugar over high heat until the liquid is reduced by half and the consistency is like syrup. Cool.

Add the wine vinegar, salt, and lemon juice, and mix well.

Meanwhile, cook the bacon until crisp. Remove from heat and allow to cool slightly. When slightly cooled, add dressing to bacon and drippings, and heat again.

Pour hot mixture over the spinach and toss well. Serve immediately with freshly ground black pepper.

4 to 6 servings.

CABBAGE SALAD

1 head white cabbage, chopped
½ cup sliced almonds (lightly
    toasted)
½ cup sesame seeds (lightly
    toasted)
6 scallions, chopped

DRESSING

4 tablespoons sugar
1 teaspoon salt
1 teaspoon white pepper
½ cup rice wine vinegar (or
    apple cider vinegar)
¾ cup salad oil

Mix chopped cabbage with scallion in a medium-to-large salad bowl. Add dressing and toss, then add almonds and sesame seeds, toss again, then serve.

Scandinavians and Germans love cucumbers. We eat them in salads, stuffed with meats and rice, in soups—about any way you can imagine.

CUCUMBER SALAD #1

2 medium cucumbers
2 tablespoons cider vinegar
2 tablespoons water
4 tablespoons sugar
1 teaspoon salt
1 teaspoon fresh dill, minced
  (½ teaspoon dried dill)

Peel cucumbers if the skins are tough, then slice very thin. Mix together remaining ingredients and add to cucumbers.

    Chill thoroughly before serving.

4 servings.

CUCUMBER SALAD #2

2 medium cucumbers, peeled
  and sliced thin
1 teaspoon salt
4 tablespoons cider vinegar
¼ cup raisins
4 tablespoons water
¾ cup sour cream
2 teaspoons onion, grated
1 teaspoon parsley, chopped
white pepper to taste

Mix sliced cucumbers with salt, water, and vinegar. Refrigerate for 2 to 3 hours, turning occasionally. Drain well.

    Plump raisins in hot water, simmer for 2 minutes, cool, and drain.

    Combine sour cream, onion, parsley, and pepper, and mix gently with drained cucumbers.

    Sprinkle raisins on top of cucumber salad.

SHRIMP SALAD

½ cup mayonnaise
½ cup sour cream
1 to 2 tablespoons ketchup or
  cocktail sauce
3 to 4 tablespoons sherry
1 pound cooked bay shrimp
2 stalks of celery, chopped fine
¼ cup parsley, chopped fine
2 scallions, chopped fine
¼ pound mushrooms, sliced
  thin
½ teaspoon dill
salt and pepper to taste
lemon juice to taste

Stir together mayonnaise, sour cream, ketchup or cocktail sauce, and sherry.

Add shrimp, celery, parsley, scallions, and mushrooms, stirring well.

Add dill, stir well, then taste. Add salt and pepper and lemon juice to taste.

Serve on lettuce leaves garnished with hard-boiled eggs, asparagus spears, tomato wedges, or artichoke hearts.

Chef Joe Sanchez has been with Pea Soup Andersen's for over 25 years. He learned the recipes for the Buellton kitchen from Juliette and has faithfully kept many of the same recipes available for customers. At home he prepares wonderful Mexican meals. The following is his version of tuna salad.

MEXICAN TUNA SALAD

1 8-ounce can of white tuna,
    drained
1 tablespoon onion, chopped
    fine
1 avocado, peeled and diced
2 jalapeño chiles, chopped very
    fine
1 medium tomato, diced small
¼ head lettuce, shredded
2 tablespoons cilantro, chopped
¾ cup mayonnaise
1 teaspoon lime juice (lemon
    can be substituted)
salt and white pepper to taste

Crumble tuna into small pieces and place in a bowl. Add all the other ingredients, and toss gently, being careful not to mash avocado, tomatoes, and lettuce.

Serve on lettuce leaves, garnished with sliced avocado, tomatoes, and cucumbers, or fresh fruit.

4 to 6 servings.

HIGHWAY BILLBOARDS
HELPED MAKE PEA SOUP FAMOUS

The following article, written in 1956, was not quite accurate in saying that travelers had been intrigued for 32 years by painted bulletins leading to Buellton and Andersen's Pea Soup. The bulletins were actually begun in the 1930s, but they definitely helped to make Pea Soup Andersen's famous.

For 32 years now, travelers along western highways have been intrigued by painted bulletins announcing road distances, usually in the hundreds of miles, to a tiny California village.

Those bulletins, together with a soup recipe, have built one of this State's more famous institutions, the landmark known as Andersen's Pea Soup Restaurant. And Buellton, on Highway 101 in the Santa Ynez Valley—a hamlet so small that motorists normally would be expected to pass through without noticing it—has become known far and wide today as a result.

People in faraway Denver, Colorado, read one outdoor advertisement which says: "1650 miles to Buellton." Residents of Phoenix, Portland and Salt Lake City, as well as those in all parts of California, see similar panels, and they are among the thousands who come to lunch and dine at Andersen's.

Ads Built Business

"Unquestionably," says Robert T. ("Pea-Soup") Andersen, the Stanford-educated proprietor, "the use of this advertising medium has been responsible in a great part for the wonderful business that we now enjoy."

So effective does he find his bulletins, he adds, that "in recent years we have had to reduce our summer season showing in order to cut down our business to the volume that we can satisfactorily take care of in our restaurant." He increases the number of bulletins during the eight off-season months to keep business level.

POULTRY AND PASTA SALAD

½ pound pasta twists or shells
⅓ cup minced red onion or
    scallions
1 small can sliced black olives
1 medium bell pepper, seeded
    and chopped
½ medium-size cucumber,
    peeled, seeded, and chopped
2 cups cooked leftover chicken
    or turkey, or smoked chicken,
    turkey, or duck
1 6-ounce jar marinated
    artichoke hearts, drained
    (optional)
tomato wedges and parsley for
    garnish

VINAIGRETTE DRESSING

¾ cup olive oil or salad oil
⅓ cup white wine vinegar
1 or 2 cloves garlic, minced
1 tablespoon Dijon-style
    mustard
1 teaspoon fresh or ⅓ teaspoon
    dried each: basil, marjoram,
    oregano, and thyme
salt and freshly ground pepper
    to taste

Cook pasta in boiling water until *al dente* (cooked but slightly firm to teeth), pour into a drainer, pour cold water over it, and drain it again.

Place pasta and the rest of the ingredients, except for the garnish, into a large salad bowl. If using artichoke hearts, cut into pieces and save marinade to use in dressing.

Mix dressing together and mix with salad. Allow salad to cool in refrigerator for several hours or overnight before serving.

Serve on lettuce leaves with garnish.

Green Goddess Dressing is good served with chilled cooked fish, shrimp, or with any green salad. This recipe makes 2 cups.

GREEN GODDESS DRESSING

1 cup mayonnaise
½ cup sour cream
2 tablespoons chives or green
　onion, finely chopped
2 tablespoons parsley, finely
　chopped (squeeze parsley for
　juice first)
2 or 3 anchovy fillets, finely
　chopped
½ teaspoon salt
1 tablespoon tarragon vinegar
1 tablespoon fresh lemon juice
1 garlic clove, minced
freshly ground black pepper

Combine all ingredients, and refrigerate for several hours. The juice from the parsley will give it a light green color.

The following dressing is great with fresh fruit. By adding 2 tablespoons of minced onion, it is very nice with green salads or pasta salads.

POPPY SEED DRESSING

1 cup honey
1 tablespoon salt
3 tablespoons vinegar
1 tablespoon Dijon-style
  mustard
½ cup salad oil
2 tablespoons poppy seeds
2 tablespoons lemon juice
2 tablespoons pineapple juice

Beat together all ingredients except salad oil. Mix well until salt is dissolved.

Gradually add salad oil. Beat until it thickens (you can run it through the blender if you wish).

Makes 1¾ cups dressing.

HONEY MUSTARD DRESSING

1 cup mayonnaise
1½ tablespoon white vinegar
1½ teaspoons salt
2 tablespoons sugar
¾ teaspoon white pepper
2 ounces salad mustard
2½ ounces honey
2 ounces salad oil
1 tablespoon parsley, chopped
1 tablespoon onion, chopped
  fine

Mix first seven ingredients in mixer at medium speed for 1 to 2 minutes, until well blended.

Slowly add salad oil; continue mixing.

Add chopped parsley and onion.

Refrigerate for 24 hours before using.

Fruit vinegars have been quite the rage in the United States for the past few years. We've been using them in Europe for a very long time. You don't have to spend a lot of money to buy fruit vinegars as they are quite easy to make.

I have given you the recipe for raspberry vinegar, but you can substitute other berries or fruits for the raspberries. You can also double or triple this recipe and make some gifts or store it in a cool dark place for your own family. Vinegars keep indefinitely if kept in a cool, dark place.

RASPBERRY VINEGAR

2 cups fresh raspberries
2 cups white wine vinegar (or
white distilled vinegar)

Place raspberries in a glass container. Mash slightly. Cover with the vinegar. Put lid on container and keep in a cool dark place for 6 days to a week. (You can keep it longer if you want a stronger fruit flavor.)

Strain through a fine sieve or cheesecloth, discard berries, and store, covered tightly, in a cool, dry place.

Patrons dining at Andersen's Valley Inn circa early 1940s.

ENTRÉES

Saurbraten is a real favorite in Europe and with Americans as well when they're introduced to it. This is my favorite version of preparing saurbraten. Serve with potato dumplings or potato pancakes and red cabbage.

SAURBRATEN

4 to 6 pound rump roast, bottom roast, or eye-of-the-round roast
2 medium onions, sliced
½ cup carrots, sliced thin
½ cup celery, sliced thin
2 bay leaves
6 whole cloves
12 whole peppercorns
12 whole juniper berries
2 cloves garlic, chopped
3 cups red wine vinegar
1 cup water
2 tablespoons butter or fat drippings
1 teaspoon each salt and freshly ground pepper
1 heel of a loaf of rye bread
2 tablespoons brown sugar

Season the meat with salt and pepper, and place into a large bowl or crock. Add all the other ingredients except butter and rye bread. Let the meat marinate, covered for 5 to 7 days in the refrigerator. Turn once or twice daily.

Remove meat and wipe dry. In a heavy Dutch oven or casserole, heat the butter or fat, add the meat, and brown on all sides.

Add marinade and vegetables. Cover and simmer for 2 ½ to 3 hours or until meat is tender.

Toward the end of the cooking, add the bread.

Remove meat to a platter and keep warm.

TO MAKE GRAVY

¹⁄₄ cup butter
¹⁄₄ cup flour (approximately)
2 cups marinade from cooking meat
sugar to taste
4 ounces red wine (optional)

In a large saucepan heat the butter. Add flour and cook, stirring constantly for 4 to 5 minutes, or until light brown.

Slowly add the marinade, stirring constantly. Add the wine and simmer until the sauce has the consistency of heavy cream. Strain and keep warm.

The sauce is to be pungent with just a touch of sweetness. Adjust the sauce with sugar to taste.

Cut the meat across the grain and serve with a little sauce. Pass rest of the sauce at the table.

Serves 6 to 8.

In Scandinavia and in Germany we like to combine meats with fruits. The following recipe uses a pork tenderloin that is pot-roasted and stuffed with apples and prunes. It is a typical Sunday entrée when the family is all together to enjoy visiting and dining as a group.

POT-ROASTED PORK TENDERLOIN STUFFED WITH FRUITS

2 pork tenderloins
1 teaspoon sugar
salt and freshly ground pepper
2 cooking apples, sliced, cored,
    and thinly sliced
10 large prunes, soaked, halved,
    and pitted
4 tablespoons butter
5 tablespoons cold water
1/3 cup light cream
2 tablespoons each butter and
    flour
pomegranate jelly (or currant
    jelly)

Split pork tenderloins lengthwise without separating the two halves, and pound the meat flat. Sprinkle each tenderloin with salt, pepper, and sugar. Place prunes and apples over the tenderloins. Then roll each tenderloin up carefully, starting at one of the shorter ends. Tie the rolls securely with string.

In a heavy, flameproof casserole, brown the tenderloins in butter, being careful not to loosen stuffing. Remove the pork rolls from the pan. Add the cold water to the casserole, and, using a wooden spoon or spatula, scrape the bottom of casserole clean. Pour in cream. Return the rolls to the casserole, cover, and simmer over low heat until the meat is tender, about 30 minutes.

Lift the rolls out of the casserole, place on a serving dish, carefully remove string, and keep meat warm.

In a saucepan, melt butter and flour together, stirring constantly until flour is lightly cooked. Add a little more butter if necessary. Mix into the juices in the casserole, and stir until thickened. Adjust the seasoning and flavor to taste with pomegranate or currant jelly. Pour some of the sauce on the pork rolls and serve the rest on the side.

Serves 6.

To prepare a good schnitzel you should use only top-quality milk-fed veal. All the fat must be trimmed and all tissue removed. Slices from the center of the rump are best. Use ¼-inch slices, about 4 to 5 ounces per person. Pound each slice as thin as possible. So, all you have is good, pure veal cutlet—that's a schnitzel! You can use pork, but wiener schnitzel is always made with veal.

Lemon is a must with wiener schnitzel. It enhances the flavor. Serve slices of lemon on top of the meat or serve lemon wedges on the side.

WIENER SCHNITZEL

4 4- to 5-ounce veal slices,
   pounded to ⅛ inch
½ cup flour
1 teaspoon salt
2 eggs, beaten
1½ to 2 cups fine, dry bread
   crumbs
½ cup butter plus ¼ cup butter
½ cup olive oil
2 tablespoons chopped parsley

Salt each veal slice. Dip first into flour and shake off excess. Next, dip into the beaten eggs, and finally into the fine bread crumbs, pressing crumbs well into the veal. Shake off excess.

Heat the oil and butter mixture until hot. Fry schnitzels for 2 to 3 minutes on each side, until golden brown. Remove and drain on paper towels.

Remove most of the butter from skillet. Add ¼ cup fresh butter to the hot frying pan, let butter brown slightly, and add 2 tablespoons chopped parsley. Remove from heat and pour over the schnitzel just before serving.

Garnish with lemon wedges.

A la Carte Sandwiches

HAKKE BOF MED ROD KAAL
Danish Hamburger Sandwich   1.50
with Fresh Mushrooms and Red Cabbage
Served on Onion Cheese Toast

ANDERSEN'S "Rich Boy" TRIPLE DECKER.
Ham, turkey, Swiss cheese and bacon, lettuce and
tomato on toast with French fried potatoes 1.75
COMBINATION HAM AND TURKEY 1.35
HAM AND CHEESE on Rye 1.25
CHEESE: AMERICAN OR SWISS (grilled or plain) ...... .65
TUNA SANDWICH "BELLEVUE" .... .85

Hot Pot Roast of Beef   1.50
SANDWICH
with Parsley Potatoes and Gravy

COLD BEEF or COLD HAM .... .90
COLD SLICED BREAST OF TURKEY .... .90
"B. L. T." Bacon, lettuce and tomato sandwich .... .90
"Third of a Pound" GROUND SIRLOIN BURGER.
Lettuce, tomato, pickles, olives and potato chips .... .85

Choice Grade
New York Cut Steak   2.50
SANDWICH
Served with Tomatoes and French Fried Potatoes

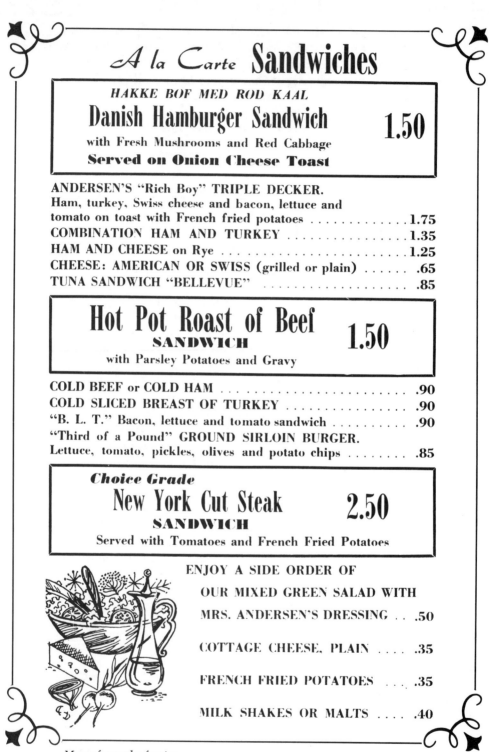

ENJOY A SIDE ORDER OF

OUR MIXED GREEN SALAD WITH

MRS. ANDERSEN'S DRESSING ... .50

COTTAGE CHEESE, PLAIN .... .35

FRENCH FRIED POTATOES .... .35

MILK SHAKES OR MALTS .... .40

Menu from the forties.

When Pea Soup Andersen's was first serving travelers, the menus had a lot of home-style entrées. Pot roast was one of the favorites. Rich and flavorful, guests felt as if they were being served the finest home-cooking without preparing the meal themselves.

BEEF POT ROAST WITH GRAVY

4 to 6 pounds chuck roast, rump roast, bottom roast, or eye of the round
1 medium onion, diced small
½ cup carrots, diced small
½ cup celery, diced small
2 teaspoons salt
½ teaspoon black pepper
¼ cup flour
1 cup water or beef stock
2 tablespoons shortening or cooking oil
1 bay leaf

Wipe beef with a clean, damp cloth, then rub salt, pepper, and flour into the meat.

Heat shortening or oil in a heavy pot or kettle, then brown meat on all sides.

Add vegetables, browning them lightly. Add the water and bay leaf, cover tightly, and simmer for 2 ½ to 3 hours. Turn the meat occasionally, adding more water if necessary. When the beef is tender, transfer to a platter and keep warm.

TO MAKE GRAVY

¼ cup butter or fat skimmed from the meat drippings
¼ cup flour (approximately)
2 cups beef stock and drippings

In a large saucepan, heat the butter, add flour, and cook, stirring constantly for 3 to 4 minutes. Slowly add the beef stock and simmer until the sauce has the thickness of heavy cream. Season with salt and pepper to taste.

6 to 8 servings.

Calf liver is very tender and delicate in flavor. When I use beef liver, I marinate the meat for an hour in milk to tenderize it and to remove some of the strong liver flavor. Serve the milk to your pets if you have any. They will enjoy it.

SAUTÉED CALF LIVER, BERLINER STYLE

1½ pounds calf liver, sliced
 ¼ inch thick
½ cup flour
¼ teaspoon salt
⅛ teaspoon freshly ground
 pepper
4 slices bacon
2 medium apples, peeled, cored,
 and sliced ½-inch thick
 (8 slices)
1 large onion, peeled and sliced
 very thin
4 tablespoons butter

In a large skillet, brown the bacon and place on paper toweling. Fry the apple slices in the bacon drippings for 1 to 2 minutes on each side or until browned. Remove and keep warm. Add 2 tablespoons of the butter and sauté the onion for 3 to 4 minutes, stirring occasionally until brown. Remove with a slotted spoon, and keep warm with the apples.

Add the rest of the butter to the skillet.

Combine the salt and pepper with the flour. Dredge the liver in the seasoned flour and sauté in the butter over medium-high heat for 2 to 3 minutes on each side.

Transfer the liver to a heated platter or individual plates. Place sautéed apple slices, onions, and bacon on top of the liver and serve immediately with mashed potatoes.

This is a truly Scandinavian special that we serve at Pea Soup Andersen's. Almost all buffets contain frikadeller. When you try it, you'll see why.

Frikadeller are traditionally served with boiled potatoes, pickled beet salad, or cucumber salad.

FRIKADELLER (DANISH MEATBALLS)

½ pound beef or veal, ground fine
½ pound pork, ground fine
½ cup soft bread crumbs or 2 slices white bread cut in small cubes
¼ cup milk
1 egg
1 teaspoon salt
⅛ teaspoon allspice, ground
1 medium onion, chopped finely
⅛ teaspoon black pepper
1 tablespoon butter
2 tablespoons shortening or oil
2 tablespoons flour
½ cup bouillon or chicken stock
½ cup milk or cream

Cook onion in butter in a large skillet until lightly browned.

Soak bread in milk and combine with onion, meats, egg, and seasonings. Mix well in a medium-size bowl.

Shape meat mixture into balls or patties.

Heat oil or shortening in same skillet. Add meatballs, cooking in two or three batches if necessary, and brown well on all sides, turning gently. Cook uncovered until cooked through.

Drain off some of the fat and add all meatballs if cooking in batches. Dust with flour, stir, and add bouillon and milk or cream.

Simmer for 5 to 7 minutes, then serve.

Makes 12 to 14 meatballs.

The following recipe for Lever Postej comes from Mrs. Alfred (Gudrun) Jacobsen, a Danish woman who provided this recipe originally for the Presbyterian Ladies Aid Cookbook in 1947. She noted in the original book that it makes a delicious sandwich spread.

LEVER POSTEJ

2 pounds fat side pork
2 pounds pork liver
1 large or 2 medium sweet
　onions
2½ cups cream
¼ cup flour
¼ cup potato flour (or potato
　starch)
3 eggs
2 level tablespoons salt
1 teaspoon sugar
½ teaspoon pepper
½ teaspoon nutmeg
ginger
allspice
cloves

Grind these ingredients together at least 5 times, then add: a pinch of each of ginger, allspice, and cloves. Mix all thoroughly together.

Line a loaf pan with strips of bacon, sides and bottom, pour in mixture, set the loaf pan in a pan of water, and bake in a slow oven, 325 degrees for 1½ hours or until firm.

Will keep well in refrigerator.

Chicken liver paté is another good buffet dish, especially if you prefer it to pork liver sausage or paté. This is very creamy and smooth.

CHICKEN LIVER PATÉ

*1 pound chicken livers, cut in
  halves
5 strips of bacon cut in 1-inch
  pieces
½ cup onion, chopped
¾ cup fresh mushrooms, sliced
3 tablespoons butter or rendered
  chicken fat
3 tablespoons brandy
½ teaspoon salt
⅛ teaspoon each: pepper,
  ground thyme, and rosemary
¾ cup butter, softened to room
  temperature*

Sauté the bacon, chicken livers, mushrooms, and onions in three tablespoons of butter over medium-high heat for 4 to 5 minutes, or until nicely browned.

Transfer to a food processor or blender. Add brandy, soft butter, salt, and herbs, and blend for 30 seconds or until very smooth. Taste, adjusting salt and pepper as desired.

Spoon into a small casserole or bowl and chill in refrigerator for 3 to 4 hours.

Serve on melba toast or crackers.

MEDISTERPØLSE (DANISH SAUSAGE)

4 pounds lean pork (shoulder,
  trimmings)
2 pounds lean veal (shoulder,
  trimmings)
2 small onions
1 tablespoon salt
1 teaspoon pepper
1 teaspoon allspice
½ teaspoon marjoram
1 cup chicken broth

Grind meat and onions coarsely together, add seasonings and chicken broth, and mix well. Put through grinder two more times.

Shape into 3-inch-round, ½-inch-thick patties and pan fry in skillet over medium heat until thoroughly cooked.

If you prefer to make link sausages, you will need a stuffing attachment for your meat grinder. Casings are available at the butcher shop.

Using the grinder attachment, feed stuffing into casing. Every 3 to 4 inches press casing together and twist to form links, or make one long rope of sausage, freeze, and cut as needed.

Makes about 24 sausages.

This is a favorite German and Scandinavian breakfast, and it's ideal for using leftovers. Roast beef, sausage, and other meats can be substituted for ham. Add green peppers, mushrooms, and shredded cheese if you like.

FARMERS' BREAKFAST

1 pound potatoes, cooked, peeled, and sliced
3 or 4 slices bacon, diced
1 tablespoon onion, diced
4 eggs
3 tablespoons milk
½ cup ham, diced
1 tablespoon chives or green onion, chopped
salt and pepper to taste

Fry bacon in skillet for 5 minutes. Add onion and potatoes, and continue frying on medium heat until nicely browned.

Beat eggs and milk together; add ham and chives. Pour over browned potatoes, stirring slowly, until eggs are cooked to your liking.

Serve with sliced tomatoes and/or sliced cucumbers.

Nell Kooyman, an employee at Carlsbad's Pea Soup Andersen's, says that the following dish is a favorite meal for a cold Dutch winter's meal.

HUTSPAT (HODGEPODGE)

2 to 3 pounds of flank steak, beef
    brisket, or short ribs
1 quart water
3 onions, sliced
4 or 5 carrots, sliced
6 potatoes, peeled and cubed
2 tablespoons butter
salt and ground pepper to taste

Place meat in a Dutch oven or kettle, cover with water, and cook for 5 minutes. Skim any foam that has risen to the surface, and then bring to a boil. Reduce heat and simmer for 1½ hours, covered.

Add vegetables and simmer another 1½ hours.

Remove meat and set aside. Drain broth from vegetables, reserving broth.

Mash the vegetables thoroughly, adding butter and broth as needed to make a thick puree. Season to taste.

Slice the meat and serve puree in deep plates with slices of meat on top.

Meatloaf was a favorite of many of the travelers stopping at Pea Soup Andersen's in the early days. It continues to be a favorite of most people as it is economical, easy to make, filling, and satisfying. This is my favorite recipe for meatloaf.

OLD-FASHIONED MEATLOAF

1 medium onion, peeled and
  diced small
2 tablespoons bacon fat or
  butter
2 teaspoons parsley, chopped
¾ cup milk
2 whole eggs
2 cups soft white bread
  (4 slices), cubed small
2 pounds ground beef or ½ each
  beef and pork
2 tablespoons ketchup
1 teaspoon salt
¼ teaspoon black pepper
½ teaspoon paprika
⅛ teaspoon granulated garlic
  (or 1 clove garlic, pressed)
¼ teaspoon thyme
½ teaspoon Worcestershire
  sauce (optional)

Preheat oven to 350 degrees.

In a medium skillet sauté the onion in bacon fat (or butter) until light brown. Add parsley, remove from heat, and let cool.

Combine milk and eggs, and bread cubes, and let stand for 5 minutes.

Mix all other ingredients together, then add bread and milk mixture.

Shape meat into a loaf or pack into a greased loaf pan.

Bake, uncovered, at 350 degrees for 1½ hours, basting off excess drippings, which can be saved and used to make gravy.

If time is of the essence, shape the meat mixture into small patties, turn them in dry bread crumbs, and fry in a mixture of butter and oil until cooked.

Serves 6 to 8.

At one time Hasenpfeffer was a regular special on the menu at Pea Soup Andersen's. Served with vegetables and noodles, in the 1940s it cost $1.00! A lot of Americans aren't sure they like rabbit, as it isn't as common here as it is in Europe. It's actually quite lean and a lot like chicken. If an older rabbit is used, I recommend marinating it first in buttermilk for a day or two to tenderize the meat. Then proceed as in the following recipe.

HASENPFEFFER

1 3-pound rabbit, cleaned, and
   cut into 10 to 12 pieces (have
   butcher prepare it if you wish)
½ teaspoon whole peppercorns
¼ teaspoon mustard seeds
6 cloves
12 juniper berries
3 bay leaves
1 large onion, chopped
½ cup water
½ cup dry red wine
1 cup red wine vinegar

Rinse off rabbit, and pat dry with paper toweling. Place the rabbit into a deep bowl. Add the rest of the ingredients. Cover and marinate in the refrigerator for 1 to 2 days, turning the rabbit several times a day.

Remove the rabbit from the marinade with a slotted spoon. Dredge the pieces of meat in ½ cup flour and set aside.

In a large skillet, heat some bacon fat, adding the rabbit when the skillet is hot. Fry over medium-high heat, browning well on each side. Transfer meat to a large kettle or Dutch oven.

Brown the remaining flour in the drippings. Add the marinade slowly to the flour, stirring until thickened. Pour over rabbit. Cover and simmer for 1½ hours until the rabbit is tender, stirring occasionally.

Remove rabbit to a serving dish. Strain sauce, then pour some over rabbit and serve the rest on the side. Serve rabbit with freshly cooked noodles.

An International Favorite

Stewed Rabbit in Wine Sauce
with Fresh Mushrooms

Lapin Marinade
(Hassenpfeffer)

$100   served with noodles
and bread and butter

PRIME GRAIN-FED RABBIT, CUT UP AND SOAKED OVER-NIGHT IN RED WINE, SPICED WITH ONION, BAY LEAF, SALT, PEPPER AND A LITTLE GARLIC. BROWNED THE FOLLOWING DAY IN BACON DRIPPINGS AND COOKED IN A DUTCH OVEN IN A WINE SAUCE TO WHICH IS ADDED FRESH MUSHROOMS AND PARSLEY.

ANDERSEN's Famous Split Pea Soup, *serving* - .20

ANDERSEN's Salad Bowl, *side order* - - - .25

ANDERSEN's Famous Hot Mince Pie - - - .15

Coffee, Tea or Milk - - - - - - - .10

Menu from the forties.

Stuffed cabbage rolls are very popular in Scandinavia, Germany, Austria, and the Eastern European countries.

STUFFED CABBAGE ROLLS

1 large head cabbage
½ pound beef or veal, ground fine
½ pound pork, ground fine
½ cup soft bread crumbs
¼ cup milk
1 medium onion, chopped fine
1 egg
1 teaspoon salt
⅛ teaspoon allspice
⅛ teaspoon black pepper
½ to ¾ cup cooked rice (optional)
¼ cup brown sugar
½ stick butter
1 cup water or bouillon

Preheat oven to 375 degrees.

Boil cabbage in salted water for 3 to 4 minutes until leaves are pliable. Drain and cool.

Core and separate leaves.

Mix the balance of the ingredients except for the butter, brown sugar, and bouillon or water.

Place a spoonful of the meat filling on the center of each cabbage leaf, folding ends to the center and rolling securely.

Butter a baking casserole dish and place the cabbage rolls close together in the pan. Add the stock or water to the rolls.

Sprinkle with brown sugar and butter, and bake for 60 minutes or until thoroughly heated.

To create a different flavor, sprinkle with whole caraway seed instead of brown sugar.

It isn't only cabbage that we like to fill with meats, rice, breads, and so forth. We also stuff cucumbers, onions, and squash. Although the fillings are the same, the textures and flavors are quite different.

STUFFED CUCUMBERS

3 large or 6 small cucumbers
4 slices bacon, diced
1 small onion, diced
1 cup water
2 tablespoons vinegar
sugar and salt to taste
same amount of meat mixture
as for stuffed cabbage rolls
(page 74)

Peel cucumbers. Scoop seeds and center pulp from cucumbers so that they are boat-shaped. Sprinkle with a little salt.

Fill center with meat filling and tie the two halves together with a string (or use toothpicks).

Brown bacon and onion lightly in a skillet. Add cucumbers, brown on all sides. Add water and simmer, covered, on low heat for 25 to 35 minutes, or bake, uncovered, at 375 degrees.

Remove cucumbers from skillet or oven and finish the sauce with a little vinegar and sugar. Add salt to taste.

Thicken the sauce with 1 tablespoon cornstarch dissolved in 3 tablespoons water, or serve as is.

Main Street, Buellton, circa 1924.

STUFFED ONIONS

8 to 10 medium onions
¼ cup brown sugar
4 tablespoons butter
1 cup water or stock
meat filling, the same as
    amount for stuffed cabbage
    (page 74)

Peel onions without cutting off root ends so that onions will remain whole. Cut a thin slice from the top of each.

Boil in slightly salted water for 10 minutes. Drain and cool. Scoop out the center of each onion leaving ⅓- to ½-inch walls.

Fill with meat mixture.

Butter a baking pan. Place stuffed onions and water or stock.

Sprinkle with brown sugar and butter. Bake for one hour at 375 degrees.

Ynez de la Cuesta submitted the following "Spanish" recipe to the cookbook of the Women of the Santa Ynez Valley. The recipe would more accurately be referred to these days as Early California food, and indeed, the de la Cuesta family was an Early California family.

CEBOLLAS RELLENAS (STUFFED ONIONS)

Boil about 8 onions in salted water until tender. When cool, separate onions into sections.

Boil about 1½ pounds of meat until tender and grind. Fry 3 well-mashed cloves of garlic in a scant tablespoon of lard and add the meat. When this is well heated, season with salt, thyme, and about ½ tablespoon of sugar. Add a little vinegar, about ⅓ cup raisins, some minced olives, mushrooms, and ¾ cup tomato sauce. Cook on slow heat until rather dry so as to be easily molded.

Make soft balls, each of about 1½ tablespoons of mixture, and wrap each in one layer of onion section. Bathe each in the following batter, and fry to a golden brown.

BATTER: For every 4 eggs, add 2 heaping tablespoons flour to the stiffly beaten whites and then add the beaten yolks.

When all are fried, put in a casserole into which has been poured the sauce; as follows:

Fry in a little lard 2 cloves of garlic, add a scant ½ cup of tomato sauce, thicken with a tablespoon of flour, add a little sugar, thyme, and salt, and the meat stock.

Cover casserole and heat thoroughly in a slow oven.

Note: If more batter is needed, make another batch. It has a tendency to separate when it stands awhile.

Leg O' Lamb

My dear Ruth:

What do the Robert Andersens eat when they eat "at home"?

Rosemary has always laughingly said that she married me because I owned a restaurant and that she would never have to learn to cook. Remarkably enough, however, she has learned to cook a few dishes incomparably well. Here is a "big" dinner which we spread quite often:

Roast Leg of Lamb
Rice
Peas
Gewurtz Traminer 1947

Mixed Green Salad with
French Dressing
Mixed Cheeses and Crackers
Inglenook Gamay
Strawberry Preserves

It's a "big" dinner because there is a lot of everything including wines, but the thing that makes the meal outstanding is the perfection of every item, be it the Roast Lamb baked with vegetables and basted with spiced wine or the story-book sauce which ensues or the Green Peas cooked in a frying pan with lettuce leaves or the Rice that no Chinaman ever cooked as well or the carefully selected greens in the Salad with a French Dressing whose ingredients are always measured almost pepper grain by pepper grain to insure repeated excellence.

I am asking Rosemary to write out the details of the mesmeric passes which she makes in preparing her Leg of Lamb.

Very truly yours,
Robert T. PEA SOUP Andersen, President

My dear Ruth:
One for your book!
For us it is Leg 'o Lamb and the only reason I dare tread along with your recipe angels . . . my husband taught me to cook it.

All meals in our house start, of course, with

Cup of Split Pea Soup
Mixed Green Salad
Leg of Lamb
Rice
French Peas
Cheeses, Jam and Crackers
Wines:
Gewurtz Traminer
Inglenook Gamay

Leg o' Lamb:
We like a small one — 4 to 5 lbs.
We like it pink — Preheated oven 325.
Wipe with damp cloth, rub well with flour, salt, coarse ground pepper and garlic inserts.
I use a shallow roasting pan with rack — no lid.
Cut 2 tomatoes in fourths

3 carrots in halves
2 brown onions in fourths
Small branches and hearts of celery
Sprigs of parsley
Sprinkle dry rosemary on top of roast.
Place in oven — two hours cooking time.
After ¾ hour add one cup hot water.
After 1½ hour add one cup hot dry white wine.
I make a roux of butter and flour for thickening sauce.
Remove roast to hot platter.
Pour all juices and cooked vegetables through sieve into small pan. Grind vegetables for pulp into same pan. Let set, then skim all fat. Reheat sauce adding meat juices from platter. Use roux for thickening and taste for seasoning . . . a little more white wine perhaps? We like to saute a few fresh mushrooms in butter and add to sauce.
Hope you like it!
Rosemary Andersen

From the Santa Ynez Valley News (see page 140).

Carlsbad employee Billie Thurman has shared her favorite lasagne recipe with us. She says she once served this to a group of people, including one very hungry football player. Seven people ate half the lasagne; the football player ate the other half! Be forewarned: This is a good recipe to serve young people with large appetites. Just make certain you make plenty.

LASAGNE CASSEROLE

MEAT SAUCE

1½ pounds ground beef
1 clove garlic, minced
1 teaspoon whole basil
1 teaspoon salt
1 1-pound can tomatoes
2 6-ounce cans tomato paste
10 ounces lasagne noodles

Brown meat slowly; spoon off excess fat. Add remaining ingredients and simmer, uncovered ½ hour, stirring occasionally.

Cook noodles in a large pot of boiling water until tender, following instructions on package. Drain, and rinse in cold water.

FILLING

3 cups ricotta or creamy cottage
  cheese
½ cup grated Parmesan or
  Romano cheese (or mixture
  of both)
2 tablespoons parsley flakes
2 beaten eggs
2 teaspoons salt
½ teaspoon black pepper
1 pound mozzarella cheese,
  sliced very thin

Preheat oven to 375 degrees.

Mix the first 6 ingredients. Place half the cooked noodles in a 13 × 9 × 2-inch baking dish; spread with half the cheese filling. Cover with half the meat sauce, and top with half the mozzarella cheese. Repeat layers.

Bake for 30 minutes or until bubbling hot.

Remove from oven and allow to stand 10 minutes before serving.

Serves 12 normal people—
2 hungry football players.

This is another of Joe's good Mexican dishes. This is best prepared on a bar-b-que but can be made on the stove if necessary.

CARNE ADOBADA (OLD MEXICAN STYLE)

1½ pounds lean meat, cut in
 fine slices (bottom round is
 ideal)
¼ cup water
¼ cup vinegar
4 tablespoons paprika
pinch of ground cloves
½ teaspoon garlic granules or 3
 cloves fresh garlic, minced
1 teaspoon cayenne pepper
pinch of thyme
pinch of salt
1 avocado, sliced
1 or 2 onions, sliced
french rolls, split, buttered, and
 toasted just before eating

Mix water, vinegar, paprika, cloves, garlic, cayenne, thyme, and salt together to create a sauce.

Spread sauce on slices of meat with a brush, applying to both sides of meat. Place meat on a dish, cover with plastic wrap, and allow to rest in refrigerator overnight.

When ready to serve, cook over a grill, in a broiler, or in a skillet with a little oil to prevent meat from sticking. Cook for desired length.

Serve meat in french rolls with slices of avocado and onions on top.

Pea Soup Andersen's president, Chuck White, has a recipe he developed years ago that has served him well entertaining by the bar-b-que from college days to the present. The name "Bunyan Burgers" is derived from the size of each meat pattie—enough for Paul Bunyan.

CHUCK WHITE'S BUNYAN BURGERS

3 pounds lean ground beef
4 or 5 eggs
2 cups shredded or crumbled
  cheese such as cheddar,
  mozzarella, Monterey jack,
  blue, or Danish
About ¾ to 1 cup each: chopped
  onion, chopped fresh
  tomatoes, diced fresh
  mushrooms
6 french rolls or hamburger buns
  (optional)
salt and pepper to taste

Mix eggs and meat in a mixing bowl. Add salt and pepper to taste.

Divide meat into 6 portions, and flatten into large, thin patties.

On the center of each meat pattie, place ⅓ cup cheese plus a spoonful of the onion, tomatoes, and mushrooms.

Form the meat around the centers so that filling is completely covered, and flatten until meat is in reasonably shaped rounds.

Broil or bar-b-que to taste, making certain meat is cooked long enough to melt the cheese and heat the condiments.

Serve with rolls if desired.

Steak tartare is raw minced beef, reshaped into a steak, and served uncooked with a raw egg yolk on top, and with chopped onions, capers, anchovy fillets, and seasonings served on the side. Each person can prepare his or her own according to taste.

This recipe is the way I like to prepare it at home. The steak tartare is placed on top of french bread and eaten like an open-faced sandwich.

It is very important to use the best-quality beef, freshly ground the same day it is served.

BEEFSTEAK À LA TARTARE

1½ pounds lean and trimmed sirloin steak of beef tenderloin
4 egg yolks
2 or 3 tablespoons onion, chopped fine
1 tablespoon capers
4 anchovy fillets, minced
2 tablespoons parsley, chopped fine
½ teaspoon Worcestershire sauce
½ teaspoon salt
¼ teaspoon freshly ground pepper
lemon wedges
crisp french bread or toast
2 pickled cucumbers or dill pickles
lettuce leaves

Finely grind the beef or chop with a sharp knife (or have your butcher prepare it).

In a bowl combine the ground steak, onion, parsley, egg yolks, capers, anchovy fillets, salt, and pepper.

Shape into 4 patties, place on a lettuce leaf on a chilled plate, and garnish with lemon wedges and dill pickles.

Serve with french bread or toast.

The Santa Ynez Valley is known for a special cut of meat called the "Tri-Tip." It is the bottom sirloin or butt cut next to the top sirloin and is available in approximately a 100-mile radius of Santa Ynez. Although its origin as a cut of meat is uncertain, there is some feeling that it was introduced by the Rancheros Vistadores, a group of roughly 800 horsemen who ride single-file through the valley each May to the Mission Santa Ynez where they are blessed by the mission priests. There is always a bar-b-que afterwards, and the Tri-Tip is the featured meat.

BAR-B-QUED TRI-TIPS

Make small slashes all around the meat, then fill with pieces of garlic. Baste well with melted butter, then salt and pepper to taste. Bar-b-que meat over hot mesquite or other wood and serve cooked to taste.

Finnan haddie is smoked and salted haddock. Like many other European foods, this popular way of preserving fish came to the United States with immigrant families. It can be prepared in many ways. The following dish can be prepared ahead and then heated and browned just before serving.

FINNAN HADDIE BAKED WITH CREAM

1 pound finnan haddie
1½ cup cream, hot
3 tablespoons butter
2 tablespoons flour
¼ cup bread crumbs, dry
1 bay leaf
1 tablespoon parsley, chopped
1 pinch each: salt, pepper, thyme, and basil

Melt the butter in a saucepan. Add flour and cook over medium heat for 4 to 5 minutes.

Add hot cream, stirring until thickened and smooth. Add seasonings and simmer for 3 to 4 minutes.

Place finnan haddie in buttered ovenproof casserole. Strain the cream sauce and pour over the fish. Sprinkle with bread crumbs and a little butter, and bake at 375 degrees for about 15 to 20 minutes or until the top becomes nicely browned.

Garnish with chopped parsley and serve immediately.

FISH FILLETS
WITH LEMON SAUCE

1½ pounds fillet of flounder,
  halibut, or seabass
1½ cups fish stock*
½ pound bay shrimp, cooked
1 teaspoon shallots, chopped
  (optional)
fresh dill or parsley for garnish

Place fish fillets and shallots in a
shallow saucepan. Add fish
stock, cover, and simmer for 8 to
10 minutes.
  Remove fish and place on a
heated platter. Pour sauce over.
Garnish with shrimp, dill, or
parsley. Serve with lemon sections and boiled potatoes.

LEMON SAUCE

1½ tablespoons butter
2½ tablespoons flour
½ cup cream
1 cup fish stock from poaching
  fish (above)
1 egg yolk
2 tablespoons cream
salt and white pepper to taste

Melt butter in saucepan over
medium heat. Stir in flour, then
add cream and fish stock gradually, stirring constantly. Simmer
for 6 to 8 minutes.
  Mix remaining cream and egg
yolk together. Add lemon juice
to sauce, then add cream and egg
mixture to sauce, stirring well.

*Instead of fish stock, you can squeeze juice of 1 lemon and mix with 1 cup
water or chicken stock. Place over fish and add 1 tablespoon butter.

BAKED FLOUNDER WITH CRAB

3 to 4 large flounder fillets (1
  pound) or other firm-fleshed
  white fish fillets
¼ pound butter
salt
Worcestershire sauce
lemon juice

STUFFING

1 cup crabmeat
2 tablespoons butter
1 small onion, chopped fine
2 cloves garlic, minced
1 stalk celery, chopped
½ teaspoon salt
¼ teaspoon white pepper
1 tablespoon parsley, chopped
1 egg
1 cup cornflakes, crushed
1 tablespoon mayonnaise
pinch of thyme

Preheat oven to 375 degrees.

Sauté onion, garlic, and celery for 4 to 5 minutes. Cool. Mix rest of the ingredients of stuffing together.

Slit a pocket in each fish fillet. Sprinkle it with a little salt, Worcestershire sauce, and lemon juice. Then stuff fillets.

Melt the butter in a pan and place the stuffed flounder fillets into pan, dark side down. Brush top of fish with some of the butter, and bake, covered, for 20 to 25 minutes. Uncover and bake an additional 10 minutes. Serve on platter, garnished with parsley and lemon.

Photograph of Actual Andersen's Food Plate

"*Pea Soup*" *Andersen recommends:*

Andersen's
JOHANNISBERGER
RIESLING

Fresh Fillet of Sole

Fresh from the Santa Barbara Channel, with potatoes, vegetables and tartar sauce.

Complete Dinner . . 3.50

Andersen's Split Pea Soup

Mixed Green Salad
with Mrs. Andersen's dressing

MAIN FOOD PLATE as pictured

Bread and butter

Wine or other beverage

A delicious **ANDERSEN'S DESSERT**

Menu from the sixties.

Salmon is revered in Scandinavia. In fact, many feel that the Norwegian salmon is the finest in the world.

MARINATED SALMON

3 to 4 pounds salmon, fresh
    center cut
½ cup salt
⅓ cup sugar
1 teaspoon white peppercorns,
    crushed
fresh dill sprigs

DRESSING

¼ cup olive oil
2 tablespoons lemon juice
1 teaspoon mustard
½ teaspoon salt
¼ teaspoon pepper

Clean fish, removing bones. Divide the salmon into 2 fillets and dry with a cloth.

Mix salt, pepper, and sugar and rub into fish. Place ½ of the dill in the bottom of a dish. Place one piece of salmon, skin-side down, in dish, and sprinkle with spices and dill sprigs. Place the other piece on top, skin-side up.

Cover with a weighted board and refrigerate for 1 to 1½ days.

Remove the spices and dill and cut into slices. Serve coated in the dressing with boiled potatoes.

Serves 6 to 8.

POACHED SALMON

2 pounds salmon

STOCK

1 quart water
1 cup dry white wine
  (optional—if not using use
  bouillon)
¼ cup white vinegar
1 tablespoon salt
10 peppercorns
1 medium onion, sliced thin
1 small carrot, sliced
1 stalk celery, sliced
2 bay leaves
1 whole lemon, sliced thin (save
  half of lemon for garnish)
5 dill sprigs
parsley for garnish

Combine all ingredients except salmon and garnish into a kettle, and boil, covered, for 10 minutes.

Now place salmon into stock, covering fish. Bring to a boil, then simmer for 12 to 20 minutes, depending on the thickness of the fish. Remove carefully and drain.

Serve with the cooked onions, carrots, and celery, and garnish with the lemon slices and parsley. This dish is good with boiled potatoes as well. They can be cooked with the stock.

To the uninitiated eel sounds gruesome. Not so at all! When eel is cooked, it has a texture and flavor not unlike chicken. The Danes love eel and especially enjoy it fried in bread crumbs. This baked eel recipe is quite similar. If you are buying eel from a fish market or butcher, have the salesperson skin and clean the eel for you.

BAKED EEL

1 eel (2 to 2½ pounds), skinned
   and cleaned
1 teaspoon salt
½ teaspoon pepper
3 tablespoons butter
1 tablespoon lemon juice
½ teaspoon Worcestershire
   sauce
2 eggs, beaten
¾ cup bread crumbs

Cut eel crosswise into 2-inch pieces, then rub with salt, lemon juice, and Worcestershire sauce. Allow eel to marinate in mixture for 15 minutes.

Dip eel pieces into beaten eggs and then into the bread crumbs. Place into a well-buttered baking dish, and dot with the remaining butter.

Place into oven and bake at 425 to 450 degrees, basting frequently. Add a little hot water, if needed, to keep eel moist. Bake for about 20 minutes.

Serve hot or at room temperature with boiled potatoes and mayonnaise or sharp sauce (sauce recipe next page).

SHARP SAUCE

1 hard-boiled egg yolk
1 raw egg yolk
½ teaspoon mustard
¼ teaspoon dry mustard
1 teaspoon parsley, chopped
¼ teaspoon salt
1 teaspoon lemon juice
¾ cup whipped cream
dash each of white pepper and
    sugar

Press cold boiled egg yolk through a fine sieve into a small bowl. Add raw egg yolk and seasonings. Mix well. Fold whipped cream into mixture very carefully. Serve on side of baked eel.

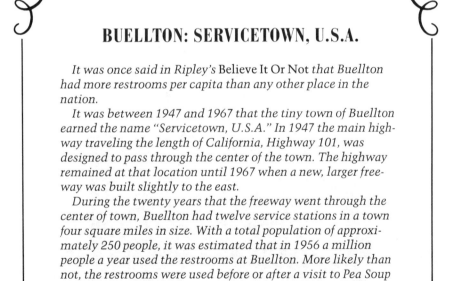

BUELLTON: SERVICETOWN, U.S.A.

It was once said in Ripley's Believe It Or Not *that Buellton had more restrooms per capita than any other place in the nation.*

It was between 1947 and 1967 that the tiny town of Buellton earned the name "Servicetown, U.S.A." In 1947 the main highway traveling the length of California, Highway 101, was designed to pass through the center of the town. The highway remained at that location until 1967 when a new, larger freeway was built slightly to the east.

During the twenty years that the freeway went through the center of town, Buellton had twelve service stations in a town four square miles in size. With a total population of approximately 250 people, it was estimated that in 1956 a million people a year used the restrooms at Buellton. More likely than not, the restrooms were used before or after a visit to Pea Soup Andersen's for a bowl or two of the famous split pea soup.

ALMOND GINGER SHRIMP

1 pound medium shrimp,
   uncooked
4 ounces (1 cube) butter
2 garlic cloves, minced
1 ounce brandy
1 ounce amaretto
½ teaspoon ginger, ground
1 tablespoon parsley, chopped
1 teaspoon shallot, minced
   (optional)
3 tablespoons almonds, sliced
   and toasted brown

Peel and de-vein shrimp.

Heat butter, garlic, and shallots in a skillet over medium heat for 1 to 2 minutes. Do not brown.

Add shrimp and cook 3 to 4 minutes until opaque, stirring occasionally. Add brandy, amaretto, and ginger. Simmer for one more minute.

Just before serving add parsley and almonds.

Serve hot with rice and garnish with lemon wedges.

4 to 6 servings.

This was a very popular item on the Pea Soup Andersen's menu for many, many years. It was served every day until the Andersen's sold the restaurant to Vince Evans, at which time fried chicken was placed on the menu and the Chicken Forester became a "special" served once or twice a month. Chicken Forester is served in individual baking dishes, but at home you can serve it in one large baking dish or casserole.

CHICKEN FORESTER

2 frying chickens, cut into pieces
1/2 cup flour
1/2 teaspoon salt
1/4 teaspoon white pepper
1/4 teaspoon granulated garlic
cooking oil
1/2 pound mushrooms
2 cups chicken gravy (recipe on
   page 95)
1/2 cup sherry wine
10 to 15 olives
chopped parsley

Rinse chicken pieces and wipe dry. Combine flour, salt, pepper, and garlic. Dredge chicken pieces in flour mixture.

In a large, heavy skillet, pour 1/2 inch of cooking oil. Heat over moderately high heat. When hot, place chicken pieces, skin-side down, in hot fat, and fry, uncovered, for about 15 minutes on each side. You may need to have two pans cooking chicken at one time so that chicken isn't crowded into pan.

When well browned, remove, drain on paper toweling, and place into a 2-inch-deep baking dish. Place pieces close together in one layer. Preheat oven to 350 degrees.

Sprinkle chicken with 2 tablespoons of sherry wine. Mix the rest of the sherry with the chicken drippings and bring to a boil. Simmer for 15 minutes. Add sliced mushrooms and ripe olives, and pour sauce over chicken.

Bake chicken, covered, for 20 to 25 minutes.

Before serving, sprinkle with chopped parsley.

Here is the home-style fried chicken we serve at our retaurants.

HOME-STYLE FRIED CHICKEN

2 frying chickens, cut into pieces
⅔ cup flour
1 teaspoon salt
¼ teaspoon white pepper
¼ teaspoon granulated garlic
¼ teaspoon paprika
1 egg
½ cup milk
oil or shortening for frying

Rinse the chicken pieces and pat dry with paper toweling.

Mix the flour with the salt, pepper, garlic, and paprika, and place into a paper bag. Combine the egg and milk and beat slightly.

Dip the chicken pieces in egg and milk batter, then into the flour mixture, a few pieces at a time. Shake bag to coat the chicken.

Pour ½ inch of cooking oil into a large, heavy skillet, and heat over moderately high heat. Place pieces of chicken, skin-side down, in hot fat, and fry, uncovered, 15 or 20 minutes on each side, adjusting heat if necessary, so that chicken doesn't brown too fast. Turn chicken once during cooking. If you wish, have 2 skillets going at once so that chicken gets cooked more quickly.

Drain chicken pieces on paper towels and serve with chicken gravy.

CHICKEN GRAVY

4 tablespoons drippings from
* chickens*
4 tablespoons flour
2 cups chicken stock
¼ cup light cream
salt and pepper to taste

Skim most of drippings from the fried chicken, leaving 4 tablespoons of fat in the pan. Stir in flour and stir until smooth.

Slowly stir stock into the flour mixture, mixing constantly until gravy is smooth and boiling.

Add the cream and season to taste with salt and pepper.

Makes about 2 cups gravy.

Chicken is really a popular dish in American homes these days as it is low in fat and is also very economical. The following three recipes are "fancy" ways to prepare chicken. They aren't very difficult, however, and they help provide variety. You can serve chicken several times a week from recipes in this book, and each way is totally different from the others.

CHICKEN WITH CREAMY MUSTARD SAUCE

2 whole chicken breasts, boned and skinned (4 halves)
3 tablespoons butter
3 to 4 tablespoons Dijon mustard
1 teaspoon shallots or onion, chopped fine
¼ cup dry white wine
½ pint heavy cream
flour for dredging
salt and freshly ground black pepper
1 teaspoon fresh tarragon (½ teaspoon dried, crumbled)
fresh parsley for garnish

Pound the chicken breasts between sheets of waxed paper until they are about ½ inch thick. Season with salt and pepper and spread about half the mustard on each side of the breasts. Dredge in flour.

In a large skillet, heat the butter, add the chicken, and brown over moderately high heat, about 3 to 5 minutes on each side.

Add shallots to the skillet, sauté briefly, and add wine.

Cook until liquid is nearly evaporated, scraping loose any bits of meat stuck to the skillet.

Add the rest of the mustard, tarragon, and heavy cream. Simmer for 1 to 2 more minutes. Add more mustard if necessary, and adjust seasonings. Garnish with parsley when served.

4 servings.

For a completely different taste but equally as good a dish, omit mustard and tarragon and use 1½ teaspoons curry powder instead.

Beautiful Soup, so rich and green,
Waiting in a hot tureen!
Who for such dainties would not stoop!
Soup of the evening, beautiful Soup!
Soup of the evening, beautiful Soup!
                    Lewis Carroll, 1832–1898

CHICKEN FRANCINE

2 whole chicken breasts, boned
   and skinned (4 halves)
2 slices of smoked ham, cut in
   half
2 slices mozzarella cheese, cut
   in half
1 tablespoon chives or scallions,
   chopped
2 eggs, lightly beaten
½ pint heavy cream
1 teaspoon shallots or onion,
   finely chopped
¼ cup sherry wine (or broth)
flour for dredging
salt and freshly ground black
   pepper
3 tablespoons butter

Pound the chicken breasts between sheets of waxed paper until about ¼ inch thick. Do not split the meat.

Season meat with salt and pepper. Place a half slice of ham and a half slice of cheese in the middle of each breast. Sprinkle with the chives or scallions and then fold breast over and pound one or two times to seal.

In a large skillet heat butter. Dredge chicken lightly in flour and then dip into the beaten eggs. Brown the chicken on both sides, about 10 to 12 minutes. Transfer to a heated platter, and keep warm.

Add shallots to the skillet and sauté briefly. Add wine and then the heavy cream. Cook the liquid over high heat until reduced to about ½ cup and pour sauce over chicken.

4 servings.

Served with rice pilaf, brown rice, or even a blend of wild rice and brown rice, this is an exciting meal for guests or for a romantic candlelit dinner.

BREAST OF CHICKEN WITH ARTICHOKES

2 whole chicken breasts, boned and halved
½ pound mushrooms, sliced
1 can (8 ounces) artichoke hearts, quartered
flour for dredging chicken
1 teaspoon shallots or onion, chopped fine
⅔ cup dry white wine (or chicken broth)
3 tablespoons butter
1 tablespoon capers
1 teaspoon parsley, chopped
1 teaspoon lemon juice
salt and freshly ground pepper to taste

Skin the chicken breasts, sprinkle with salt and pepper, and dredge in flour.

In a large skillet heat 3 tablespoons of butter. Add the chicken and brown on both sides. Lower heat, then add the mushrooms. Cover and cook for about 10 to 15 minutes. Stir occasionally.

Remove chicken breasts and place on warmed platter. Keep warm.

Add shallots to the skillet and sauté briefly. Add the wine. Cook over high heat until the liquid is nearly evaporated, scraping loose any particles of meat.

Stir in the artichoke hearts, lemon juice, capers, and chopped parsley.

Pour sauce over chicken breasts, and serve.

4 servings.

Len Jepsen is a native of the Santa Ynez Valley who grew up in Solvang. He remembers when everyone left their doors unlocked, including the shopkeepers. Whenever anyone needed an item from a shop that was closed, they simply left a note and the money on the counter. Those days are long gone, however, and Len prefers to stay out in Santa Ynez now, which is still rural and quiet.

Len worked for years as a painting contractor for Pea Soup Andersen's. As "Pea-Soup" frequently remodeled or changed the restaurant design, he was kept busy. In his spare time he developed quite a reputation as a bar-b-que chef, and now no Santa Ynez function is complete without Len Jepsen's bar-b-qued beans and chicken. His recipes are quite simple but delicious.

LEN JEPSON'S BAR-B-QUED CHICKEN

Marinate chicken pieces in a mixture of Wishbone Italian Dressing and blush wine (he often uses Gallo Rosé for large bar-b-ques), for at least 6 hours or preferably overnight. Partially cook chicken by steaming it in chablis that has been seasoned with prime rib seasoning. Then bar-b-que until tender and browned on the outside.

LEN JEPSON'S CHILI BEANS

For each pound of cooked chili beans use 1 pound hamburger meat, 2 or 3 onions, 1 medium can chilis, chopped, and prime rib seasoning to taste. Cook at least 1 day in advance to allow the flavors to mellow.

Another of Joe Sanchez's excellent Mexican-American dishes.

JOE SANCHEZ'S CHILI BEANS

1 pound pink beans
1 large onion, chopped
¾ cup tomato puree
2 tablespoons chili powder
1 teaspoon cumin
½ teaspoon black pepper
1 tablespoon garlic finely
   chopped, or
1 tablespoon granulated garlic
⅛ teaspoon salt
1½ pounds coarsely ground beef
   or pork

Cook the beans in a heavy kettle in water until tender.

Brown the meat in a skillet, remove with a slotted spoon, and sauté onion in the drippings until slightly brown.

After the beans are cooked, remove water so that you can see the top of the beans. Add the sautéed onion, tomato puree, chili powder, cumin, pepper, garlic, and salt.

Simmer for about 30 minutes, then add browned meat.

Cook at a simmer for an additional 15 minutes.

4 to 6 servings.

Highway billboard.

SIDE DISHES

Cabbage is a favored vegetable all through Europe, partly because it is available even during long and often very cold winters. The Scandinavians and the Germans are especially fond of red cabbage. I have first given a recipe for Danish red cabbage and then German red cabbage as there are differences in preparation. Both are delicious, however, and especially as a side dish to our rich-flavored meats.

DANISH RED CABBAGE

3 pounds red cabbage
¼ cup vinegar
2 tablespoons butter
¼ cup water
1 tablespoon sugar
¼ cup applesauce
2 tablespoons pomegranate jelly
salt and pepper to taste

Wash the cabbage thoroughly, discarding the core and imperfect leaves. Cut or shred into thin strips.

Cook in butter for 3 to 4 minutes. Add water, vinegar, sugar, and applesauce.

Cover and simmer for 45 minutes. Add pomegranate jelly and simmer for an additional 15 minutes.

Add salt and pepper to taste.

This dish is best prepared a day in advance and then reheated.

GERMAN RED CABBAGE

3 pounds red cabbage
1 large onion, peeled and diced
   small
4 slices bacon, diced small
4 tablespoons red wine vinegar
2–3 medium apples, peeled,
   cored, and diced small
1 tablespoon sugar
¼ cup water
1 bay leaf
⅛ teaspoon cloves ground, or
   5–6 whole cloves
salt and pepper to taste
2 tablespoons flour mixed with
   ⅔ cup water

Wash the cabbage thoroughly, discarding the core and imperfect leaves. Cut or shred cabbage into thin strips.

In a large kettle sauté diced bacon until light brown. Add onion and sauté an additional 4 to 5 minutes. Add cabbage and the rest of the ingredients except flour and water, and cook covered for 60 minutes.

Mix flour and water until smooth and add slowly to boiling cabbage, stirring well, and simmer for another 15 minutes.

This dish, like the Danish red cabbage, tastes much better if prepared a day in advance and reheated.

Serves 6 to 8.

Vince Evans had a great deal of energy and at least as much good intent, but occasionally even the best of intentions went awry.

Vince and his wife, Marge, bought the old adobe home that was part of the de la Cuesta Spanish land grant. There was a problem with the hillside behind the house which blocked the view or sunlight, so Vince decided to blow up the hill and landscape the level ground. Unfortunately, he was a little overzealous with the dynamite, and he blew up part of the house as well and cracked parts of the floor and the walls.

They decided to move to the Alisal ranch at that point, but he kept the adobe house. When he set up the wild animal exhibit in what is now the parking lot for the Buellton restaurant and motel, he turned the adobe home over to the Derbys, owners of the animals. Evelyn Buell had reason to go over to the old adobe one day and was quite taken aback when she saw the large aviary stretched across the living room and animal skins stretched over couches and chairs. But the coup de grace was when she went into the bathroom and discovered a kangaroo living in the bathtub. She said that it distressed her to see a historical landmark being used to house animals, even if they were exotic.

WHOLE FRIED ONIONS

4 medium onions
1 quart water
2 tablespoons butter
1 teaspoon brown sugar
½ teaspoon salt
½ cup stock or water

Peel onions. Boil in water for about 10 minutes. Drain.

Brown butter in skillet or Dutch oven.

Add onions, sprinkle with sugar and salt, and brown. Add stock or water and simmer, covered, until soft.

Serve with roasted beef.

HONEY GLAZED CARROTS

3 tablespoons butter
¼ cup honey
1 teaspoon sugar
¼ cup orange juice (fresh if possible)
4 cups carrots, peeled and sliced
1 teaspoon salt
⅛ teaspoon ground bay leaves
2 tablespoons onion, chopped fine
1 teaspoon parsley, chopped

Melt butter in a skillet, add onion, and sauté briefly.

Add rest of ingredients and bring to a boil. Cover tightly, reduce heat, and cook slowly over low heat until carrots are tender, about 20 minutes. Stir occasionally.

Before serving, sprinkle with parsley.

Serves 6.

Pancakes are always a popular dish in Scandinavia and Central Europe. Although we almost always serve potato pancakes with certain roasts and meats, other types of pancakes can be served as well. If you're tired of making soup with dried split peas, you might like to try the following savory pancake recipe.

SAVORY SPLIT PEA PANCAKES

1 cup split peas, rinsed and
   drained
2 cups water
2 cups finely chopped onion
2 garlic cloves, minced
1 egg, well beaten
¼ cup all-purpose flour
1 teaspoon salt
½ teaspoon pepper
yogurt or sour cream

In a saucepan, combine split peas and water. Cover; bring to boil.

Reduce heat and simmer 30 to 35 minutes or until peas are tender. Cool slightly. Stir in onion, garlic, egg, flour, salt, and pepper.

Heat a skillet or griddle over high heat. Coat lightly with oil or shortening. Drop batter by large spoonfuls onto hot skillet; spread batter evenly. Cook until surface bubbles burst; edges will look slightly dry. Turn pancakes and cook until underside is golden. Garnish with yogurt or sour cream.

Makes about 12 pancakes or 4 servings.

Potato pancakes are delicious served with sour cream and/or applesauce. This amount makes about 16 to 18 pancakes. They are so good that it's hardly enough for 4 servings. If you're cooking for hearty eaters, you may want to double the recipe.

POTATO PANCAKES

2 pounds Idaho potatoes
2 (½ pound) small onions
1 teaspoon salt
2 eggs
¼ cup flour
⅛ teaspoon nutmeg
⅛ teaspoon white pepper
½ cup shortening or oil for
   frying

Peel and grate potatoes and onions into a bowl.*

Stir in the eggs, salt, nutmeg, and pepper. Gradually add the flour and mix well.

Heat shortening in a large frying pan until sizzling hot. Drop a spoonful of batter into it and flatten slightly.

Over medium heat brown pancakes on one side, turn, and brown on the other until crisp.

Drain pancakes on absorbent paper towel and serve at once.

*I use an electrtic grater (small holes) and get the job done in 2 minutes. You could also use a food processor if you have one that grates evenly.

ANDERSEN'S famous green **SPLIT PEA SOUP** (all vegetable)

Soup Combination 95¢

Bread and Butter: Danish Onion-Cheese Bread and Danish Pumpernickel

Soup: *All you can eat!*

Beverage: Vin Rosé or Milk Shake or Coffee, Tea, Milk, Buttermilk

A LA CARTE: Single Bowl of Soup with Crackers Only . . 50¢

Menu from the sixties.

DANISH POTATOES

1½ pounds potatoes (about 6
  medium potatoes)
½ pound bacon
2 tablespoons butter
3 tablespoons vinegar
1 tablespoon chopped parsley
salt and pepper to taste

Cook unpeeled potatoes in boiling water. Drain, remove skins, and cut into cubes or slices.

Cut bacon into squares and fry crisp in butter. Add potatoes, vinegar, and parsley.

Season with salt and pepper and toss lightly until well mixed and hot.

Serves 4 to 6.

Caramelized potatoes are a typical side dish in Scandinavia.

CARAMELIZED POTATOES

3 tablespoons granulated sugar
⅓ cup butter
2 pounds potatoes, peeled,
  boiled, and drained
salt and pepper to taste

Put sugar in a heavy frying pan over low heat. Stir gently until sugar melts and turns golden.

Add butter and allow to melt.

Stir in potatoes, and heat, turning potatoes gently until covered with glaze.

Serves 6.

SCALLOPED POTATOES WITH DANISH CHEESE

6 medium to large potatoes
2 cups creamy Havarti cheese or
   other creamy Danish cheese
1 cup hot milk
4 tablespoons butter
salt, pepper, and paprika to taste

Preheat oven to 400 degrees.

Oil a shallow baking dish.

Wash potatoes. Peel if desired, removing any bad-looking spots on potatoes. Slice very thin.

Place half the potatoes in baking dish. Sprinkle with cheese, small pieces of butter, and seasonings. Place the other half of potatoes in pan and cover with the remaining cheese, butter, and seasonings.

Carefully pour heated milk over potatoes, avoiding moving the cheese to one end of the pan.

Put pan in center of oven and bake for about 40 minutes or until the potatoes are tender and crusty-brown on top.

BROWNED POTATOES

2 pounds boiled potatoes (white
    or red is fine)
2 tablespoons butter
½ cup bread crumbs
½ teaspoon salt
½ teaspoon sugar

Peel potatoes and shape into small balls.

Brown butter and bread-crumbs in a medium-size skillet.

Add the potatoes and shake continuously until the potatoes are covered with bread crumbs and have browned. Sprinkle salt and sugar over potatoes, then turn a couple of times.

Place directly on plates or around the entrée on a serving platter.

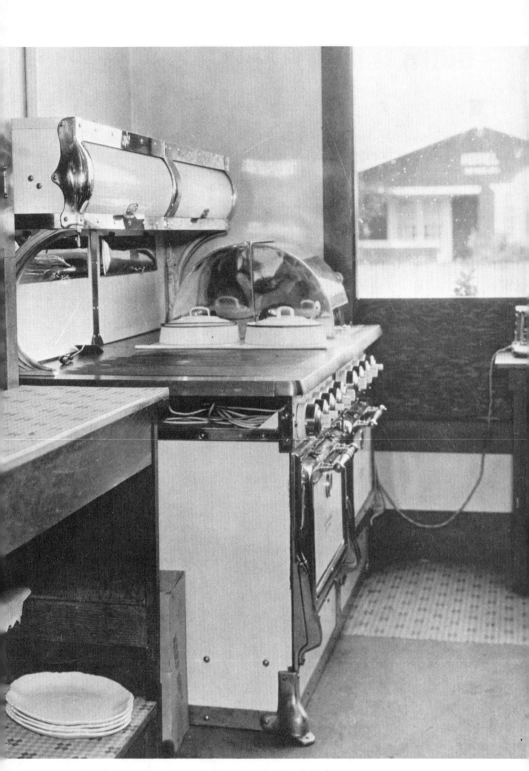

The electrical stove in Andersen's Electrical Cafe.

BREADS

When Fernando Palomino set up the Santa Nella Pea Soup Andersen's location, it was difficult to find a bakery that could produce good Danish baked goods. To solve the problem, he set up a bakery himself. The delicious onion cheese bread for which Pea Soup Andersen's is famous is one of the breads they bake daily. Here is the recipe, cut down to three loaves. Even if there are only a few people in your family, you will have difficulty keeping the bread around your house for long!

ONION CHEESE BREAD

¾ cup dry milk
2 tablespoons dehydrated onion
2 tablespoons sugar
1½ packages active dry yeast
2½ cups water, warm but not hot
8 cups flour
1½ tablespoons salt
¼ cup shortening, softened or melted and cooled
1½ tablespoons cheese powder (or ½ cup grated cheddar cheese)
3 tablespoons poppy seeds

Stir dry milk, onion, and sugar into warm (not hot!) water, then sprinkle with yeast. Let mixture stand for 5 minutes until the surface is frothy. Gently stir to moisten and soften all of the yeast.

Sift flour and salt into a large bowl. Stir in the shortening. Combine the liquid mixture with the flour, add cheese powder, and mix well until dough takes form.

Turn dough out onto a floured board. Knead dough for 5 to 10 minutes or until smooth and elastic. Place into a greased bowl.

Cover and let rise in a warm place for 30 minutes.

Preheat oven to 350 degrees.

Punch dough down and remove from bowl to floured board. Knead the dough lightly, then divide into 3 equal pieces. Shape into loaves, and place on a floured baking sheet. Cover and let rise in a warm place for 30 minutes.

Bake in oven for 45 to 50 minutes or until browned on top. Cool on racks.

Makes 3 loaves.

Most of these recipes would not taste quite the same without good rye bread. You can purchase good rye breads in bakeries, but there's nothing quite like the smell of fresh bread baking at home to lift everyone's spirits.

RYE BREAD

6 cups rye flour
2 cups all-purpose white flour
2½ cups milk
2 packages active dry yeast
1½ teaspoons salt
⅓ cup butter
¾ cup molasses
2 to 3 teaspoons fennel seed, crushed

Dissolve yeast in ½ cup warm milk. Melt butter, add remaining milk, and heat to lukewarm. Pour into a large bowl.

Add molasses and 3 cups of rye flour to large bowl. Beat well. Add yeast mixture, salt, fennel, and remaining flour gradually. Beat until smooth.

Cover bowl with towel and let rise in a warm place until double in bulk, about 2 hours.

Turn dough out onto floured board and knead well.

Divide the dough into 3 pieces and shape into loaves and place on baking sheets. Prick loaves with the tines of a fork. Let rise in a warm place, about 30 minutes.

Preheat oven to 375 degrees.

Place loaves of bread in oven and bake for about 30 minutes, or until loaves are browned and sound hollow when "thumped." Brush loaves with warm water when halfway baked, and again when they are fully baked.

Cool loaves of bread on a rack.

For those of you who are unfamiliar with aebleskive, it is a baked delight made with a pancake-like batter, cooked in a special pan that turns the aebleskive into a crusty ball, and is known as the "Danish Doughnut." As you can tell, it is a little difficult to give aebleskive an easy definition other than to tell you that it is good enough to go ahead and order the pans if you are likely to serve breakfasts and brunches to family and friends.

Aebleskive pans are available through most gourmet cookware shops or can be ordered from Pea Soup Andersen's Santa Ynez Valley Wine Center, (805) 688-5581.

AEBLESKIVE

3 eggs, separated
2 cups buttermilk
1 teaspoon sugar
½ teaspoon salt
2 cups flour
1 tablespoon baking powder
1 teaspoon baking soda
¼ teaspoon cardamom

Beat yolks of eggs with buttermilk.

Mix together sugar, salt, flour, baking powder, baking soda, and cardamom.

Beat egg whites until stiff.

Mix egg yolk-buttermilk mixture with dry ingredients. Add egg whites, carefully folding them in so that they don't break down.

Heat aebleskive pan. Put 1 teaspoon salad oil in each hole and fill completely with batter. Let bake until slightly crusty on bottom. Turn slightly with a knitting needle or skewer. Continue cooking, turning the ball to keep it from burning, until the knitting needle comes out clean when stuck in the center.

Serve aebleskive hot with powdered sugar, jam, and jelly.

In 1947 the Ladies Presbyterian Aid of the Santa Ynez Valley put together a cookbook. Evelyn Buell was the editor. Although Juliette's recipes were coveted, there was something new from Andersen's that took precedence over recipes. The following ad was on the inside of the cookbook cover.

Europe is famous for its incredible pastries: France for delicate, flaky croissants and pastries filled with butter; Germany for strudels; Austria for tortes—and Denmark for its Danish pastries. Indeed, the word "Danish" means breakfast rolls to many Americans.

The reputation for delicious breakfast sweets is well deserved. Making most Danish pastries requires some time, often not available to families where both husband and wife work. But if you have some time on a weekend or want to prepare something special for the holidays, making one of the following recipes will not only give you something good to eat, but also the pleasure of creative baking.

DANISH KRINGLE

1 package yeast
¼ cup warm milk
1 cup butter
2¼ cups flour
½ teaspoon salt
2 tablespoons sugar
2 eggs, beaten

FILLING

½ cup butter
½ cup sugar
fruit filling*
pure vanilla extract or other
   flavoring
egg white
nuts, if desired (sliced almonds
   are especially nice)

Dissolve yeast in warm milk in a large mixing bowl, stirring with a wooden spoon. Add sugar and salt to yeast mixture and blend.

In a food processor or separate bowl, mix butter and flour until it resembles fine cornmeal. Stir into yeast/milk mixture.

Add eggs slowly, stirring, until eggs have been totally absorbed into dough.

Turn mixture out onto a floured board and knead, adding in more flour as necessary. Knead until dough becomes smooth and elastic, about 10 minutes.

Divide dough into 2 or 3 parts and roll each into oblong strips. Set aside.

*Cooked prune, apricot, apple, berry, or cherry fillings are perfect for kringle. Either make your own from fruits, water or juice, and sugar to taste, or use canned pie fillings. You can also make a mixture of cream cheese, a little cream to thin it slightly, sugar, cinnamon, cardamom, or other flavorings to taste, and nuts.

Cream butter and sugar together and spread on strips of dough. Spread fruit filling to which the vanilla or other flavoring has been added to about ¼ inch of sides of dough.

Fold the dough into thirds lengthwise and place on a greased baking sheet, seam-side up. Brush with beaten egg white and sprinkle with nuts or leave plain to frost after it has baked. Cover baking sheets with dish towels and set in a warm place to rise. Allow to rise for 2 hours.

Preheat oven to 350 degrees. Place sheets in oven and bake for about 20 minutes or until lightly browned. Place pans on racks to cool. Slice pastries into strips 1 to 1½ inches wide, or frost with powdered sugar and cream or a butter-cream frosting and then slice.

DANISH PUFF

1 cup butter, in 2 sections
   (2 cubes)
2 cups flour
¼ teaspoon salt
2 tablespoons cold water
1 cup boiling water
1 teaspoon almond flavoring or
   pure vanilla extract
3 eggs

FROSTING

1½ cups sifted powdered sugar
1 tablespoon butter
3 tablespoons cream
1 teaspoon pure vanilla extract
⅛ teaspoon salt

Preheat oven to 425 degrees.

Mix ½ cup butter into 1 cup flour and salt until consistency of coarse cornmeal. (This part can be done with a food processor, if desired). Add cold water and blend well. Divide dough in half and press each half onto an ungreased cookie sheet.

Pour boiling water into a saucepan and add remaining butter. When the butter melts, remove from heat and add almond or vanilla flavoring. Stir in 1 cup flour all at once. Beat smooth and allow to cool. Beat in eggs, 1 at a time, beating well after each addition.

Spread this mixture over the pastry on the cookie sheet. Bake for 15 minutes, then at 400 degrees for about 30 minutes. Watch pastry closely last 10 minutes so that it doesn't burn. Place pan on cooling rack.

Mix frosting until smooth and spreadable. Spread on puff while puff is still hot. Fruits or nuts can be used to decorate puff if desired.

Serve warm.

One of the great delights of cold European winters is the smell of freshly baked bread. Christmas stollen is high on the list of favorites, as it always brings with it wonderful memories of cold, snowy days and warm family gatherings.

CHRISTMAS STOLLEN

7½ cups all-purpose white flour, sifted
1 pound butter, room temperature
3 packages dry yeast
1½ cups warm milk (not hot)
3 eggs
2 cups sugar
1 cup almonds, chopped
1½ cups candied fruits (orange, lemon, cherries)
1 tablespoon lemon rind, finely grated
1 cup raisins
¼ cup dark rum
1 teaspoon vanilla extract
1 tablespoon melted butter
1 cup powdered sugar

Place 5 cups of flour into a large mixing bowl. Make a hollow in the center of the flour and pour yeast into the hollow. Sprinkle the yeast with a little sugar (about 1 tablespoon), and pour the warm milk over the yeast. When the yeast starts to bubble, mix the ingredients into a paste. Cover with a cloth and keep warm to rise.

In another bowl mix the butter, sugar, and eggs, until foamy.

Add the balance of flour, candied fruits, rum, and vanilla.

Blend together the dough and the butter mixture, adding a little more milk if necessary. The dough should be quite firm. Knead well, cover with a cloth, and let rise in a warm place.

Turn dough out onto a lightly floured board, and form an oval, then fold in half, lengthwise, bending the ends to form into a thick loaf. Transfer to a buttered baking sheet and let rise for 30 minutes.

Preheat the oven to 350 degrees.

Brush stollen with the melted butter and place into oven. Bake for about one hour, until golden brown.

Allow to cool briefly on pan, then transfer to a wire rack and dust several times with powdered sugar.

Stollen can be made into 2 smaller loaves if preferred.

Theresa Bohnett is a Pea Soup Andersen's employee who now works and resides in Carlsbad. She grew up in Santa Barbara, however, and her grandparents were friends of the Andersens'. Theresa offers us her delicious banana nut bread, a nice bread to serve at a buffet or for afternoon tea.

BANANA NUT BREAD

1 cup sugar
½ cup butter
2 eggs
1 tablespoon sour milk
3 bananas, mashed
1 teaspoon lemon juice
2 teaspoons baking powder
¼ teaspoon salt
½ teaspoon baking soda
2 cups all-purpose flour
1 cup nuts, coarsely chopped

Preheat oven to 375 degrees.

Beat together the first 8 ingredients, then add flour and soda. Mix well. Add chopped nuts.

Pour batter into a greased loaf pan and bake for approximately 1 hour or until loaf pulls slightly from the sides of the pan.

Cool in pan for 10 minutes, then transfer the bread to a wire rack and cool completely before slicing.

AN OUTSTANDING REVIEW
FROM DUNCAN HINES

A review in Duncan Hines' column, "Adventures in Good Eating," in the February, 1948 issue of Coronet magazine, lent even more credibility to Andersen's Valley Inn, not to mention more customers coming to Buellton to try the pea soup.

ADVENTURES IN GOOD EATING

In this feature—one of a series—Duncan Hines takes Coronet readers to some of the outstanding restaurants which are listed in his famous book, *Adventures in Good Eating*.

—THE EDITORS

DUNCAN HINES

WHEN YOU ORder a bowl of split-pea soup at Andersen's Valley Inn in Buellton, California, it is served with the fanfare that most eating places reserve for such delicacies as *crêpes suzette* or flaming-sword dinners. A cart bearing a huge tureen mounted over a burner is wheeled to your table; a white-coated attendant ladles out a bowlful of the steaming soup and sets it before you with the air of a knight offering jewels to royalty.

There's good reason for all this ceremony. Andersen's is probably the only restaurant in the country that claims to be built "on a solid foundation of split-pea soup."

It started in the early '20s when Anton Andersen, a Danish immigrant who had served as a *maître d' hôtel* in New York, decided to "retire" in California. But Andersen couldn't resist the impulse to take over a small roadside café which was being offered for lease. On his bill of fare he featured split-pea soup, prepared according to a recipe from Mrs. Andersen's French family cookbook.

Truck drivers and traveling salesmen were his first patrons. Then some of Andersen's New York customers, vacationing in California, "discovered" him, and soon limousines were parked alongside trucks outside his cafe.

Today, Anton's son, Bob, is managing the Valley Inn. He uses 20 tons of fresh peas and serves more than 200,000 bowls of the famous soup annually. In fact, his product has now been put in frozen form, for use in customers' homes throughout the country.

JOE SANCHEZ'S CORN BREAD

4½ cups flour
1 cup sugar
4 cups cornmeal
4 tablespoons baking powder
½ teaspoon salt
1¼ cup butter, melted
3 cups milk
8 eggs, beaten
¼ cup cooking oil or bacon
   drippings

Preheat oven to 375 degrees.

Combine flour, sugar, baking powder, salt, cornmeal, and butter, mixing well.

In a separate bowl, whip eggs and milk and oil or bacon drippings. Add to dry mixture. Stir until well blended.

Pour into a well-greased 9 × 14 × 2-inch baking pan and bake for 25 to 30 minutes, until bread pulls away slightly from edges of pan, or if a fork inserted in the middle comes out clean.

Cool for a few minutes before cutting into large squares. Serve with lots of butter.

Buellton employee Barbara Olsen has an unusual—and delicious—recipe for a yeasted corn bread.

YEASTED CORN BREAD

1 cup milk
½ cup butter or margarine
2 packages yeast
6 tablespoons sugar
½ cup warm water
2 beaten eggs
2 teaspoons salt
1¾ cups cornmeal
3½ cups flour

Preheat oven to 375 degrees.

Scald milk in a medium-size saucepan. Stir in sugar, salt, and butter or margarine. Cool to lukewarm.

In a large bowl, mix warm water with yeast. Stir to dissolve. Add milk mixture and eggs, then flour and cornmeal. Beat for about 2 minutes. (Batter will be stiff.)

Divide into two well-greased loaf pans.

Cover pans and allow the dough to rise to double in size, about 1 hour.

Bake for about 35 minutes, or until tops are firm and browned.

Allow to cool on a rack for 15 minutes or so before turning out of pans.

The following recipe is a classic example of the pioneering quality of women living in the country and making-do during hard times. A lot of these old recipes have been discarded as life has gotten easier, but they probably should not be forgotten. This recipe is from the cookbook prepared by the women of Santa Ynez Valley, submitted by Ednah Smith of Nojoqui.

FRIED BREAD

A Quaker Oats box with lid punctured is fine for all leftover bread to dry without mildewing. Even the hardest will quickly soften in water. Squeeze dry as possible into the size dish you wish to serve, not too fine. Have iron frying pan hot, with bacon drippings, 2 or more tablespoons. Put damp bread into it and sprinkle generously with salt and pepper and fry like potatoes until browned.

When Rob Andersen was in his early twenties, he was working as a manager for the family business. Pea-Soup had been giving him a hard time about his 1948 pickup truck, as he felt it wasn't the appropriate vehicle for a manager of the business to drive. He wanted him to sell the pickup and use a company station wagon. Rob, on the other hand, was attached to his truck and didn't much want to part with it for a station wagon, dignity or not.

Having grown up around celebrities who frequented the restaurant and bar, Rob was not at all intimidated one evening when he saw Kim Novak sitting in the bar. She was his idol and he wasted no time going over to her table and joining her. In retelling the story now, however, he laughs at his priorities. "I think my opening line was, 'What kind of car do you drive, Miss Novak?' She said she drove a station wagon that the movie lot provided her. She said she had some kind of car of her own as well. It wasn't anything impressive. So then I asked her what she thought of a 1948 pickup, and did she think it was undignified for me to be driving it. She thought it was perfectly reasonable to have the truck. Boy, that gave me some ammunition for my case!"

This is a showy breakfast treat for family and friends.

HOLSTEIN PANCAKE

1 cup flour, sifted
1 cup milk
4 eggs
⅓ cup butter or bacon drippings
¼ teaspoon white pepper
½ teaspoon salt

Preheat oven to 425 degrees.

Put eggs in blender and mix for 1 minute. While keeping the blender running, slowly pour in the milk, then add flour and seasonings. Continue mixing for another 30 seconds.

Place butter into a heavy iron skillet and put into the oven. Remove when butter is all melted, and pour batter into the skillet. Return to the oven and bake until pancake is fluffy and brown, approximately 20 to 25 minutes.

Serve at once with butter and syrup or jam.

CHILDREN'S MENU

Hap-Pea's Special
LUNCHEON or DINNER

For the Youngsters

1.50

Complete Dinner

TEENY-WEENY CUP OF SPLIT PEA SOUP

Choice of Special Children's Portion of Following

1. **BAKED HAM,** Sweet Potato, Vegetable
2. **POT ROAST OF BEEF,** Noodles, Vegetable
3. **FILLET OF SOLE,** Potato, Vegetable
4. **GROUND ROUND STEAKBURGER PATTY,** Potato, Vegetable

A BIG* Serving of Ice Cream
and a Glass of Milk
or
A BIG* Creamy Milk Shake

*
*In case Mamma reads this for you,
a wink from her to us means really
not such a big serving.*

Menu from the sixties.

These pancakes can also be fried on a griddle. Serve with lingonberries or jam.

BACON PANCAKE

¾ cup flour
2 eggs
1 cup milk
1 teaspoon butter, melted
½ pound bacon, sliced and cut
    into 1-inch pieces
½ teaspoon sugar
pinch of salt, pepper

Preheat oven to 400 degrees.

Sift flour into a bowl. Add salt, pepper, and sugar. Add eggs and milk gradually, stirring until well blended. Add butter last.

Fry bacon in skillet until crisp. Pour off fat.

Pour batter over bacon. When brown, turn and bake for 10 minutes.

Serve immediately.

DANISH DUMPLINGS

1 cup water
¼ cup butter
1 cup flour
¼ teaspoon salt
3 eggs
pinch of white pepper and
   nutmeg
1 teaspoon parsley, chopped fine
   (optional)

In a heavy medium-size sauce-pan, combine butter and water. Bring to a boil. Stir in the flour, mixing well until the mixture is smooth.

Remove from heat and cool slightly. Add seasonings and eggs, one at a time, beating briskly.

Drop by teaspoon into hot, but not boiling, broth.

Simmer for 6 to 8 minutes, uncovered, and then for 2 to 3 minutes covered.

Serve with chicken stews, meat stews, or soups.

People enjoy the bread pudding we serve at Pea Soup Andersen's so much that we make it at each of our locations every day. Because we often have day-old Danish pastry, we always use that in our pudding, which makes it very rich. Leftover bread can be substituted. Adjust sweetening to taste.

HONEY BREAD PUDDING

2 1/4 cups milk
1/3 cup sugar
4 eggs
2 tablespoons honey
1/4 teaspoon cinnamon
1/8 teaspoon nutmeg
1/2 teaspoon pure vanilla extract
4 cups Danish pastry (1 or 2
    days old, cut into cubes)
1/4 cup raisins

Preheat oven to 350 degrees.

Mix first seven ingredients together, stirring well.

Fill a buttered casserole with the cubed Danish pastry and raisins mixed together.

Pour the custard mix over the pastry and let it stand for 15 minutes.

Place casserole in a large shallow pan and pour hot water 1 inch deep into the pan.

Bake, uncovered, for about 45 minutes or until knife inserted in the middle of the pudding comes out clean.

Cool slightly and serve with whipped cream.

4 to 6 servings.

La Buvette was a colorful French bistro-style bar with a mural above the bar that depicted a typical French street scene.

When La Buvette was moved the mural was taken down and stored in a garage.

Rob says that when he was about nine or ten he had a fort in the adjoining garage. The mural was precisely the right height for him and so he took a drill and drilled out the eyes of the people painted on the mural. This way he could hide behind the mural and observe the action in the next garage.

Needless to say, there was a bit of commotion when the drilled eyes were discovered, and the mural was never again hung on the walls of Pea Soup Andersen's.

DESSERTS

CHOCOLATE RUM PUDDING

1 egg
½ cup sugar
4 tablespoons cocoa
⅔ cup cream
2 tablespoons dark rum
1 tablespoon gelatin, soaked in
   2 tablespoons water
1¼ cups heavy cream, whipped

Mix egg, sugar, cocoa, and cream in top of double boiler and cook until thick, beating constantly. Remove from heat. Add gelatin and rum.

Place mixture in bowl and refrigerate, stirring every 10 minutes until cold. Fold in whipped cream, then pour into mold, rinsed in cold water.

Refrigerate 3 to 4 hours before unmolding.

Garnish mold with whipped cream flavored with vanilla. Serve with fancy cookies.

This is another very popular dessert at Pea Soup Andersen's. All the ingredients except for the ice cream are available from Andersen's wine cellar.

DANISH CHERRY WINE SUNDAE

1 part Cointreau liqueur
2 parts simple syrup*
4 parts Andersen's Danish
    cherry wine
8 parts Andersen's cherry
    preserves

Mix all ingredients together and refrigerate overnight.

Serve over French vanilla ice cream.

*Simple syrup: Dissolve 1 cup sugar in ½ cup boiling water. Allow to cook 3 minutes.

LEMON FROMAGE

8 eggs, beaten separately
2 cups sugar (or less according to
  taste)
juice of 3 lemons
rind of 1 lemon
2 tablespoons gelatin
1 cup water

Beat yolks of eggs with sugar. Add lemon juice and rind, then the gelatin dissolved in hot water.

Fold in egg whites and chill. Serve with whipped cream.

VANILLEKRANSE (VANILLA SPRITZ COOKIES)

1½ cups butter
2¼ cups sugar
2 eggs, beaten
1½ teaspoons pure vanilla
  extract
3½ cups flour
½ cup finely chopped almonds

Preheat oven to 325 degrees.

Cream butter and sugar. Add the rest of the ingredients, and mix until smooth.

Put dough in cookie press and press onto greased cookie sheet in small wreaths, or other shapes.

Bake in oven about 10 to 12 minutes, or until golden-brown.

This is a delicious treat, not too sweet, but very appealing, that has its counterpart all through Europe.

OLD WORLD KREPELCHEN

½ pound butter, softened
1 cup sugar
½ teaspoon pure vanilla extract
1 grated lemon rind
juice of ½ lemon
4 eggs
3½ cups flour, sifted
1 teaspoon baking powder
¼ cup rum
2 to 3 cups oil for frying
¾ cup sugar or powdered sugar
  for coating krepelchen

Mix all ingredients except for oil and extra sugar. Add the eggs, one at a time, beating well.

If the dough is too soft for rolling, add flour until it becomes firmer.

Roll dough out on a floured board until it is about ¼ inch thick.

Cut dough into strips 3 inches long and 1 inch wide. Cut a 1 inch slit in the center of each strip. Pull one end through the slit and pull slightly on both ends to get a bow-like effect.

Deep-fry bows in hot oil, a few at a time, until golden brown. Remove bows with a slotted spoon and transfer to paper toweling.

Put sugar in a small bag, add Krepelchen a few at a time, and shake until coated.

Serve freshly made, if possible.

Makes about 3 dozen.

In the late 1940s or early 1950s, another cookbook came out in the Santa Ynez Valley. This book was compiled by Ruth Gordon from columns she wrote for the *Santa Ynez Valley News* in Solvang. The book begins:

> *How it started—When Ladies are having their hair curled it seems their talk turns to food instead of glamour. One day when the recipes were flying thick and fast over the bobbie pins it occurred to me it would be fun to share these tasty ideas—so that's how this column was born. Valley hostesses will share their favorite menus with you and sometimes one of my own will appear.*

In a section devoted to "Holiday Goodies," Juliette Andersen had submitted:

DREAM BARS

Light oven and set at slow 325 degrees.

Grease a shallow pan measuring about 10 by 13 inches.

Cream together until light and fluffy *6 tablespoons butter or other shortening, ½ cup light brown sugar, lightly packed.*

Beat in *2 tablespoons light cream.*

Sift before measuring *1 cup all-purpose flour.*

Add gradually to sugar mixture. Put in prepared pan, spreading to the corners. Bake 15 minutes.

Meanwhile beat until light, *1 egg.*

Add gradually *1 cup brown sugar, lightly packed.*

Stir in mixture of *3 tablespoons light cream, 1 teaspoon vanilla, ¼ teaspoon salt.*

Fold in a mixture of *1½ cups shredded coconut, 1 cup broken nutmeats.*

Spread over top of batter, which has baked 15 minutes. Bake 25 minutes longer or until top is browned. Cool, cut in bars.

Makes about 2½ dozen.

As the employees sent in recipes to share in our cookbook, we got a recipe from Theresa Bohnett (whose grandparents were friends of Anton and Juliette), that is almost identical to the one provided to the Santa Ynez Valley cookbook by Juliette! The only difference is that her recipe is called "Lemon Dream Bars" and contains the following glaze:

DREAM BAR GLAZE

2 teaspoons grated lemon rind
2 tablespoons lemon juice
1 cup sifted powdered sugar

Mix ingredients well, then spread over cookies that have cooled but have not yet been cut into bars. Allow to cool and harden (put in refrigerator for an hour if you wish) before cutting into bars.

Nell Kooyman, a Carlsbad employee, shares with us her recipe for appelbeignets, or apple fritters. She says, "The Dutch New Year's celebration is never complete till this dessert-like snack is served after midnight with a good cup of coffee." Actually, this is a wonderful recipe to serve any time of the year when good tart apples are available. It makes a very nice addition to a brunch or afternoon treat.

APPELBEIGNETS (APPLE FRITTERS)

4 cooking apples, preferably
   green, peeled, and cored
2 tablespoons sugar
½ teaspoon fresh nutmeg
2 tablespoons lemon juice
fat for deep-frying
1 cup all-purpose flour
½ teaspoon salt
1 to 1¼ cups beer
powdered sugar

Slice apples in ½-inch rings. Sprinkle with sugar and nutmeg, then pour lemon juice over the apples to keep them from turning brown.

Heat oil to 380 degrees.

While the fat is heating, combine flour, salt, and ½ cup beer. Stir well, then add more beer, enough to make a smooth, rather thick batter.

Dip apple slices into batter, then fry, a few slices at a time, until they are golden-brown.

Drain on paper towels, then sprinkle well with powdered sugar. Serve warm.

Pamela Beckworth, head of the marketing department at our Carlsbad location, provided our cookbook with a real American favorite, pecan pie. Although pecan pie probably originated in the southern United States, it has become so popular that it's served just about everywhere.

PECAN PIE

1 unbaked 9-inch pie shell
2 eggs, lightly beaten
½ cup light brown sugar
½ teaspoon salt
2 tablespoons flour
3 tablespoons melted butter
1 cup white corn syrup
1 teaspoon pure vanilla extract
1½ cups pecans, broken in large
　　pieces

Preheat oven to 350 degrees.

Mix together all ingredients except for about ¾ cup of the pecans. Pour into pie shell. Press the rest of the pecans onto the top of the pie.

Bake pie about 40 minutes or until set. Cool on rack.

Serve slightly warm or at room temperature with sweetened whipped cream or ice cream if desired.

Green tomato pies are an "old-fashioned" dessert, one that was (and still is) served in farming communities where tomatoes are grown in abundance. There were two recipes for green tomato pie submitted to the cookbook compiled by the women of the Santa Ynez Valley. The following is Jeanette Lyon's recipe.

GREEN TOMATO PIE

enough green tomatoes to fill a
  pie (6 to 8)
small piece of butter (1 to 2
  tablespoons)
1 cup sugar
dash of nutmeg
1 tablespoon cornstarch
1 tablespoon vinegar or ½
  tablespoon lemon juice

Peel and slice green tomatoes to fill a pie. Stew with a little water to draw out the strong liquid. Drain this off.

Add butter, sugar, nutmeg, cornstarch, and vinegar or lemon juice. Cook until thick.

Cool before filling uncooked pie shell.

Add an upper crust.

Bake in moderate (350 degree) oven until cooked and crust is browned (about 40 minutes).

Brian Jessen, head of maintenance at Pea Soup Andersen's in Carlsbad, comes originally from our midwestern corn and wheat belt. Although he and his wife now live in California, they still enjoy cooking hearty meals and baking their own bread just as they did growing up on a farm. Brian's family are of Danish heritage, and he was pleased to share some traditional Danish recipes for this book. The following two recipes are made with apples, perfect for cold autumn evenings and winter holidays.

PAPER BAG APPLE PIE

1 unbaked 9-inch pastry shell
4 large baking apples, sliced
½ cup sugar
2 tablespoons flour
½ teaspoon nutmeg
½ teaspoon cinnamon
2 tablespoons lemon juice

TOPPING

½ cup sugar
½ cup flour
½ cup butter

Preheat oven to 425 degrees.

Mix together all ingredients except pastry shell, and fill pastry shell.

To make topping, in a medium-size mixing bowl, place sugar and flour. Cut butter in with fingers or fork until mixture resembles coarse cornmeal. Sprinkle on top of apple mixture, spreading well to the outside of crust.

Slide pie into a heavy brown paper bag, large enough to cover pie. Fold open end over twice and fasten with a straight pin. Place on cookie sheet for easy handling.

Bake in oven for 1 hour. Remove from oven, cut open paper bag, and cool pie on a rack.

Serve with whipped cream or ice cream.

MOTHER'S DANISH APPLE CAKE

2 cups fine, very dry bread
   crumbs
½ cup sugar
½ cup melted butter or
   margarine
3 cups very thick, sweetened
   applesauce (cook down sauce
   if necessary)
1 cup whipping cream, whipped
   and sweetened
currant jelly if desired

Combine bread and sugar. Melt butter in large skillet. Add crumb mixture. Heat at very low temperature until light golden brown, stirring often.

Butter a deep 1½-pint bowl. Make a layer of ½ cup bread crumbs in bottom of bowl. Follow with a layer of applesauce. Repeat until crumbs and applesauce are used, ending with a layer of crumbs. Press the layers together with a small plate.

Cover bowl and chill overnight.

Unmold on serving plate. Frost with whipped cream. Slice to serve. Top each serving with jelly, if desired.

Variation: Add 1 teaspoon red cinnamon candies to applesauce. Heat, stirring, until candies are dissolved.

Makes 10 to 12 servings.

Vince Evans supported the endeavors of the local 4-H and other farm programs. He always bid on the prize cattle and sheep, paying a handsome price for his purchases. When Pea Soup Andersen's opened in Santa Nella, Vince asked Fernando Palomino, the manager of the Santa Nella site, to attend the local auction and to bid on the prize animals for him. Fernando had never gone to an auction before and had no idea of what he was supposed to do. Ever faithful to his employer, Fernando and his wife Ginger bought cowboy boots and hats, and went to the fair. They watched the bidding through the early part of the show, figured out more or less what they were supposed to do, and by the time the champion animals were brought into the arena, they were going strong.

The locals were very interested in the two strangers bidding on their prize animals, so they came over to introduce themselves and began buying Fernando and Ginger drinks. By the end of the auction they were quite drunk, and the next day, Fernando recalls, he had a terrible hangover.

Vince called Fernando and asked how the auction went. Fernando said he guessed it had gone all right. Evans asked him how much he spent. Fernando replied that he wasn't really sure, but it might be as much as $8,000. Not batting an eyelash, Evans said, "That's fine. Just send me the bill."

Ten years later Fernando is still attending auctions, bidding on the local champion animals. Now, however, he has gotten totally caught up in the bidding; usually another employee attends with him to keep track of the costs and to hold him back when he gets too carried away by the excitement.

Patricia Rain, coordinating editor of this cookbook and admitted cho-
coholic, feels that *every* American cookbook should have a good recipe for chocolate cake. "Chocolate cake is at least as American as hot
dogs and apple pie, and I'll bet most Scandinavian and other European
families have (or wished they had) a favorite recipe they use for special events. So this is my contribution to the Pea Soup Andersen's
cookbook."

She says that the layers can be filled with strawberry or raspberry
jam along with the truffle frosting to add a very European touch to the
cake.

SOUR CREAM CHOCOLATE CAKE

MIX TOGETHER

*1½ cups thick sour cream (or
cream that has turned)*
1½ cups sugar
2 teaspoons pure vanilla extract
2 tablespoons butter, melted

SIFT TOGETHER AND ADD

Scant 2¼ cups unbleached flour
½ cup cocoa (unsweetened)
1½ teaspoons baking soda
½ teaspoon salt

BEAT IN, ONE AT A TIME

4 eggs

Preheat oven at 350 degrees.

Pour into 3 8-inch greased cake
pans or 1 8-inch square greased
baking pan, and bake at 350 degrees
for about 20 minutes or until top
springs back when touched and
toothpick comes out clean when
inserted into center of cake.

Cool cakes on racks for 20 minutes before inverting and removing
from pans. When completely cool,
cake rounds can be layered, and
frosted. Square cake can be frosted
on top in pan, or inverted onto a
platter, sliced in half horizontally,
and filled and frosted.

TRUFFLE FROSTING

1 cup heavy cream or
   evaporated milk
1 cup granulated sugar
4 ounces unsweetened
   chocolate
1 cube butter
1 tablespoon pure vanilla
   extract

Place cream or evaporated milk and sugar into a heavy saucepan and bring to a boil, stirring constantly. Reduce heat slightly, and allow mixture to cook for 8 minutes.

Remove mixture from heat, and add chocolate, broken into pieces, and butter. Stir until chocolate and butter have completely melted and are blended.

Add vanilla extract, blend well, and then place mixture in refrigerator.

Allow mixture to chill until it begins to thicken. Beat mixture with a wooden spoon or balloon whisk until it becomes thick and light. Fill and frost cake with frosting. If using jam, spread a thin layer of chocolate frosting on cake layer, then cover layer with about ⅓ cup raspberry or strawberry jam. Place on next layer and repeat process. Place the top layer on, and frost entire cake with frosting.

Serves 12 regular cake eaters, fewer if they like chocolate.

Billie Thurman, a Pea Soup Andersen's employee at Carlsbad, has an almost-no-fail cheesecake recipe that has won her accolades from past employers. She made it as a birthday gift for a boss a number of years ago. His comment was, "I consider myself a connoisseur of fine cheesecake, and this is the finest I have ever tasted." From then on she was expected to produce cheesecake for every birthday party at her office. The "almost-no-fail" isn't because the recipe is difficult. Billie says she was slipping the cake back into the oven for its last baking one evening when the pan struck the oven door and cake fell all over the oven, the floor, and her. The next day she brought a chocolate cake made from a mix to the party! So as long as you're careful, you'll have a perfect cake each time you follow this recipe.

BILLIE THURMAN'S CHEESECAKE

1 teaspoon cinnamon
¼ cup granulated sugar
1 teaspoon shortening
¼ cup melted butter
1¼ cup crushed graham
  crackers

Grease a 10-inch spring form pan with shortening. Combine cinnamon, sugar, crackers, and butter, and cover sides and bottom of pan with the crust.
  Preheat oven to 375 degrees.

FILLING

4 8-ounce packages cream
  cheese, room temperature
1 cup sugar
6 eggs
2 teaspoons pure vanilla extract

Mix together until smooth using an electric beater or food processor. Pour into pan and bake 50 minutes. Remove and cool 15 minutes in pan.

TOPPING

1½ pints sour cream
½ cup sugar
2 teaspoons pure vanilla extract

Increase oven temperature to 425 degrees.

Mix the topping ingredients together and pour over cake.

Bake another 10 minutes.

Remove from oven and cool on a rack until cold. Place in the refrigerator for an additional 3 to 4 hours before removing the ring and serving.

This cheesecake can be also covered with a can of cherry pie filling or fresh strawberries mixed with a jar of strawberry glaze. Most fresh fruits or berries are nice to decorate the cake with or to serve on the side.

Chuck White's wife, Eileen, has a treasured family recipe, dedicated to her Grandma Kate. According to Eileen, this is a "never-miss cake" bound to please everyone. They serve it for holidays and other special occasions.

VIVIAN'S OLD WORLD HONEY CAKE

¾ cup honey
3 eggs
¾ cup vegetable oil
1 heaping teaspoon baking
   powder
1 heaping teaspoon baking soda
1 cup sugar
1 jigger rye
½ cup strong black coffee
1 jigger club soda or any
   effervescent soda
3 cups flour
sprinkle of spices such as
   allspice, ginger, nutmeg, and
   cloves
almonds or walnuts for
   decoration

Preheat oven to 300 degrees.

Grease a large bundt pan or springform pan.

Put all the ingredients in a large bowl. Mix for 15 minutes or until everything is completely blended and the batter is light.

Place almonds or walnuts into creases in bundt pan. If using a springform pan, either place the nuts in the bottom of pan, or add to top of batter after it has been added.

Pour the batter into the pan. Place in middle of the oven. Bake for approximately 1½ hours, or until an inserted toothpick or knife blade comes out clean.

Cool for about 15 minutes, then invert onto serving plate.

Serves about 16.

Mary Newman, restaurant manager of the Carlsbad location, originally comes from England. Her holiday tradition includes making Christmas puddings, the delicious steamed puddings in a traditional English holiday. The puddings take 2 days to prepare—one day the ingredients are mixed together. After mellowing overnight, the puddings are steamed. This recipe makes 2 1-pound puddings or 1 2- pound pudding.

TRADITIONAL ENGLISH CHRISTMAS PUDDING

½ pound currants
½ pound sultanas (golden raisins)
½ pound large black raisins
¼ pound mixed peels (lemon, orange, citron, or green and red peels)
½ pound white bread crumbs
½ pound brown sugar
½ pound prepared shredded beef suet
¼ pound whole almonds, blanched (skins removed)
½ pound all-purpose flour
¼ teaspoon salt
1 teaspoon ground nutmeg
1 teaspoon ground cinnamon
1 teaspoon allspice
grated rind and juice of 1 lemon
3 eggs
½ pint stout (malt liquor)

DAY ONE

Mix currants, sultanas, raisins, and peel together in a large mixing bowl. Stir in bread crumbs, sugar, suet, and lemon rind. Chop almonds and add to fruit.

Sift flour, salt, and spices together. Beat eggs, and add lemon juice and stout. Add flour and egg mixture to the other ingredients and mix well together. Allow to sit overnight.

DAY TWO

Grease 1 large or 2 small containers (either designed for steaming or containers that will work for steaming such as loaf pans) and fill with pudding mixture. Cover each container with parchment paper and tie securely with string.

Place container(s) in a large steamer or pot with a vegetable steamer set in it, and steam for 8 hours if one large pudding, for 6 if two. Be certain to check water level frequently.

Remove puddings from steamer, and allow to cool on racks. Remove parchment, recover with fresh, and store in a cool place.

On Christmas day steam in the same way for at least 2 hours (or put in microwave oven for 15 minutes).

Unmold puddings onto a serving platter. Dust with sugar and garnish with a holly sprig.

Serve with pouring custard (crème anglaise) or whipped cream.

This is a very dramatic end to a special meal. Be certain to read the full recipe several times, and ideally, practice this on family before trying to impress guests. It isn't difficult, but it does take a little practice to make it work well.

BANANAS FORSTER

2 tablespoons butter
4 tablespoons brown sugar
½ teaspoon cinnamon
1 tablespoon banana liqueur
1 ounce brandy or rum
2 bananas
good-quality vanilla ice cream

Mix butter and brown sugar in saucepan. Start heat and cook until lightly carmelized. Cut bananas in quarters or ¾-inch chunks. Add to saucepan and simmer for 3 to 4 minutes.

Add cinnamon and liqueur to mixture. Stir well. Add rum or brandy to the top of mixture, but do *not* stir.

Very carefully set rum or brandy on fire. Spoon mixture over individual servings of ice cream while banana mixture is flaming.

Serves 4.

CHOCOLATE POPCORN

6 cups freshly popped corn
1 cup coarsely chopped pecans
1 cup roasted peanuts
8 ounces semisweet chocolate

In a double boiler melt the chocolate over low heat.

Place popcorn in a large bowl. Add pecans and peanuts. Mix well. Add hot melted chocolate and mix carefully using a wooden spoon.

Turn mixture out onto a greased sheet of waxed paper. Press flat until mixture is about 1 inch thick.

Cool until mixture is hard. Cut into bars with a sharp knife. Wrap in plastic wrap to store—if you have any left.

SANTA NELLA
I-5, 60 miles South of Stockton
(209) 826-1685

BUELLTON
Highway 101, North of Santa Barbara
(805) 688-5581

CARLSBAD
I-5, 30 miles North of San Diego
(619) 438-7880

WHAT'S HAPPENING AT PEA SOUP ANDERSEN'S

Pea Soup Andersen's currently has three locations serving both highway travelers and local residents. Buellton is the home of our original site, with Santa Nella and Carlsbad joining in the late 1970s and early 1980s. All three locations have restaurants with seating capacities of up to 700 guests. Banquet facilities, meeting rooms, and full catering services are also available.

Each of our Pea Soup Andersen's locations offers a variety of specialty shops featuring freshly baked goods, unusual gourmet foods, quality dinner wines as well as our Danish dessert wines, and gift items. The Santa Ynez Valley Wine Center at our Buellton location carries the finest wines of the valley and has a wine-tasting bar.

Throughout the year we have festivals and celebrations, many of which are seasonal. In the spring there are flower shows, Mother's Day parties, spring fests, and wine tasting; in the summer, luaus, country music festivals, chili cookoffs, and Fourth of July bar-b-ques. In the autumn we have harvest wine and food parties, Oktoberfest, and National Pea Soup Week celebrations; in the winter, arts and crafts fairs, community bazaars, Christmas caroling, and special holiday parties. We also have summer concerts, winemaker dinners, dinner-dance parties with name bands, and local evening entertainment.

If you want your visit to coincide with events occurring at our locations or in the nearby communities, please give us a call and we will happily help you plan your visit.

A NOTE ABOUT SOLVANG

Three miles east of Buellton and Pea Soup Andersen's lies the beautiful Danish town of Solvang. At the turn of the century it was nothing more than fields of beans planted behind the old Mission Santa Ines. This area of the valley had been bypassed in favor of the towns of Santa Ynez and Los Olivos.

In 1910, however, the Reverend J. M. Gregersen announced a plan to start a Danish colony on the West Coast in an attempt to tie immigrants together with their native Scandinavia. Central to the idea of the colony was the Danish folk school, or Atterdag. Along with the Reverend Benedict Nordentoft and Professor P. O. Hornsyld, from the Danish Grand View College in Des Moines, Iowa, Gregersen purchased 9,000 acres from the Santa Ynez Valley Development Company. The new town site was named Solvang, meaning "sunny field."

The first pioneers arrived in the spring of 1911 and began establishing homes and businesses. In 1912 the Bethania Lutheran Church was founded, and the church and Atterdag shared the same building on Alisal Road (now the Bit O'Denmark Restaurant). In 1928 the church moved to its present site on Atterdag Road, and Atterdag College was

built on a hill overlooking town in 1914, where it stood until 1970 when it was torn down.

The premise of Atterdag College was to educate students for the life that lay ahead of them. There were no examinations and no degrees. In addition to the basics, Scandinavian customs, music, and dance were stressed. Unfortunately Atterdag closed as a folk school in 1937 as it could no longer compete with "accredited" schools.

Solvang initially looked like any small California farming town until the 1940s. When Ferd Sorensen of Nebraska and his Danish wife, Gudrun, arrived in Solvang, he worked as a plumber and built houses on the side. After visiting Denmark, Ferd built his home, Møllebakken (the mill on the hill) in Danish provincial style. At the end of World War II, the late Ray Paaske saw the potential for drawing tourists to Solvang, and he asked Ferd to design the first commercial enterprises in town, again using Danish provincial architecture.

An article published in the *Saturday Evening Post* in 1946 drew the first tourists to Solvang. The story included colorful photographs of the town, families dressed in bright costumes, folk dancing during Danish Days, and so forth.

Over the years, the town has prospered from tourist trade. The Danish royal family has visited Solvang many times, and with each visit, the town has gained more celebrity. Danish Days began in 1935, but remained a small hometown celebration until 1947. The *Post* article interested so many people that the Solvang community decided to stage their celebration with an open invitation to the outside world. *Everyone* came! In 1959 Danish Days was moved to September as the summer crowds proved too much for the small town.

The town now has a thriving tourist trade year-round, with people coming to sample the delicious Danish foods and baked goods and to browse among the beautifully handmade Danish wares for sale. There is a performing arts theater that offers repertory theater in an open-air setting during the summer months, and there are numerous small celebrations at regular intervals in addition to Danish Days.

In 1985 Solvang was granted its own charter, making it the first incorporated city in the Santa Ynez Valley. From bean fields to the Danish Capital of the United States is a big leap in only 75 years.

For families visiting Pea Soup Andersen's Buellton accommodations, we highly recommend a side trip to Solvang. And as Pea Soup Andersen's roots are deep in the Danish tradition, we serve the lovely pastries made by Birkholm's of Solvang as well as several other Danish food specialties.

INDEX

E

Eel, baked, 90
Eggs
    Cebollas Rellenas (Stuffed
       Onions), 77
    Chuck White's Bunyan Burgers,
       81
    Farmers' Breakfast, 69
Entrées, 57–101

F

Farmers' Breakfast, 69
Finnan Haddie Baked with Cream,
    84
Fish Fillets with Lemon Sauce, 85
Flambé, Bananas Forster, 156
Flounder, baked, 86
Fried Bread, 128
Frikadeller (Danish Meatballs), 65
Frosting, truffle, 149
Fruit Soup, 28

G

German Red Cabbage, 105
Gravy, 59, 63
    chicken, 95
Green Goddess Dressing, 53
Green Tomato Pie, 144

H

Hasenpfeffer, 72
Herring in Sour Cream, 34
Holstein Pancake, 129
Homestyle Fried Chicken, 94
Honey Bread Pudding, 133
Honey cake, Vivian's Old World, 152
Honey Mustard Dressing, 54
Hot Potato Salad, 45
Hutspat (Hodgepodge), 70

J

Joe Sanchez' Chili Beans, 101
Joe Sanchez' Corn Bread, 126

K

Krepelchen, Old World, 139

L

Lasagne Casserole, 79
Lemon Fromage, 138
Len Jepson's Bar-b-qued Chicken,
    100
Len Jepson's Chili Beans, 100
Lever Postej, 66
Liver
    Chicken Liver Paté, 67
    Lever Postej, 66
    Sautéed Calf Liver, Berliner Style,
       64

M

Meatloaf, Old Fashioned, 71
Meats
    Bar-b-qued Tri-tips, 83
    Beef Pot Roast with Gravy, 63
    Beefsteak à la Tartare, 82
    Carne Adobada, 80
    Cebollas Rellenas (Stuffed
       Onions), 77
    Chicken Liver Paté, 67
    Chuck White's Bunyan Burgers,
       81
    Frikadeller (Danish Meatballs), 65
    Hasenpfeffer, 72
    Hutspat (Hodgepodge), 70
    Lasagne Casserole, 79
    Lever Postej, 66

ABOUT THE AUTHOR

C hef Ulrich Riedner, known as Ulli by his friends and colleagues, was born in Oldenburg, Germany. After completing high school Ulrich began an arduous three-year apprenticeship as a chef. He received his diploma from a school in Augsburg, then worked for six months in a local restaurant before joining his older brother, who was already established as a chef in Las Vegas.

Chef Riedner initially worked under his brother in the pantry, at the broiler, and as a saucier, before going to work at the Sultan's Table at the Dunes Hotel.

Chef Riedner moved through the ranks of his trade quickly. Within a few years of arriving in Las Vegas he was a chef de cuisine; within ten years he was an executive chef overseeing 80 cooks in large hotels and country clubs.

In 1974, Chef Riedner came to California as the first chef of the elegant Pisces Restaurant, located in Rancho de la Costa. Later he opened the Chez Orleans Restaurant and nightclub in Escondido where he remained until November, 1985, when he came to work for Pea Soup Andersen's as Corporate Chef.

Ulrich Riedner has participated in culinary shows, judged cooking contests, and has been the featured guest on television. He is a member of the Escoffier Society and the Chef's Association of Nevada. He lives with his wife, Francine, and their two sons.